The
happy hour

The Happy Hour

SERMONS FOR ADVENT, CHRISTMAS AND EPIPHANY
(SUNDAYS 1-8 IN ORDINARY TIME)

JAMES H. BAILEY

SERIES C FIRST LESSON TEXTS FROM
THE COMMON (CONSENSUS) LECTIONARY

C.S.S. Publishing Company, Inc.
Lima, Ohio

THE HAPPY HOUR

Copyright © 1985 by
The C.S.S. Publishing Company, Inc.
Lima, Ohio

All rights reserved. No portion of this book may be reproduced or utilized in any form or by any means, electronic or mechanical including photocopying, without permission in writing from the publisher. Inquiries should be addressed to: The C.S.S. Publishing Company, Inc., 628 South Main Street, Lima, Ohio 45804.

N85.5T

5856 / ISBN 0-89536-750-5   PRINTED IN U.S.A.

Dedication

To D. L. Holly, MYF Counselor and Educator, in whose life I saw Christ incarnated.

Acknowledgements:

To Jeanne Rouse, Jean Hedden for their typing. To Pamela and Walter Turner for their editing and final manuscript. Without these beautiful friends this book would not exist.

Table of Contents

Advent 1	It's Hard For God to Get Through to Us Jeremiah 33:14-16	9
Advent 2	Can We Pass Inspection Malachi 3:1-4	15
Advent 3	His Coming is to be Welcomed, Not Feared Zephaniah 3:14-20	21
Advent 4	The Happy Hour Micah 5:2-5a	29
Christmas Eve/ Christmas Day	Is There Any Word From God? Isaiah 52:7-10	35
Christmas 1[1,2] Holy Family	Spiritual Growth 1 Samuel 2:18-20, 26	41
Christmas 2	The Shepherd Guards His Sheep Jeremiah 31:7-16	49
Epiphany	The Narrow Way Broadens Us Isaiah 60:1-6	57
Epiphany 1 — Baptism of Our Lord	The Effect of Christ's Coming Isaiah 61:1-4	65
Epiphany 2[1,2] Ordinary Time 2[3]	Burned Out Isaiah 62:1-5	73
Epiphany 3 Ordinary Time 3	The Happy Find Nehemiah 8:1-4a, 5-6, 8-10	81
Epiphany 4 Ordinary Time 4	I'll Be Listening For My Name Jeremiah 1:4-10	89
Epiphany 5 Ordinary Time 5	The Moment of Decision Isaiah 6:1-8 (9-13)	95

Epiphany 6 **Ordinary Time 6**	*The Coming of Jesus Illuminates* *Humanity* *Jeremiah 17:5-10*	103
Epiphany 7 **Ordinary Time 7**	*Recognizing God in Our Midst* *Genesis 45:3-11, 15*	111
Epiphany 8 **Ordinary Time 8**	*Prayer: How to be Sure of Results* *Isaiah 55:10-13*	115
Transfiguration[1,2]	*How To Get a Glow on Your Face* *Exodus 34:29-35*	123

[1] Common Lectionary
[2] Lutheran Lectionary
[3] Roman Catholic Lectionary

Jeremiah 33:14-16   Advent 1

It's Hard For God to Get Through to Us

Advent requires us to experience a vision from God in whatever circumstances we find ourselves, and for that vision to bring hope and the possibilities of the coming of the King who will bring peace.

Recently I picked up the novel, *Cold Heaven,* by Brian Moore, from the public library. It was the story of Marie Davenport, a successful physician's wife who was having an affair with another doctor. Neither of these persons was religious or spiritual, and both considered Christianity sheer nonsense. One day, after Marie had met her lover, she left the motel up at Big Sur and was walking along the cliffs. Suddenly she had a vision which she described this way: "And then I felt something very strange. It was a sort of silence, as if the sea wasn't moving, as though everything was still. Then the branches of the cypresses rustled and shook, and someone came out through the trees below me. It was a young girl. She couldn't have been more than sixteen. It was a cloudy day. Did I say that? There was no sun at all and yet she was surrounded by a little golden path of light. She said to me, 'Marie, I am your mother. I am the Virgin Immaculate.' " Every time Marie told of her vision, she always prefaced and concluded it with, "I do not believe in miracles. I do not believe in the Virgin Mary. I don't believe in any religion."

Several weeks later, while she and her husband, Alex, were attending a medical convention in Europe, Alex, swimming in the Bay of Angels at Nice, was run over by a motorboat, which smashed his skull. He was rushed to the hospital, but even the skill of famous French doctors couldn't save him. He was pronounced dead and taken to the morgue. The next day his body disappeared. No one could understand it. Truly, someone must have stolen his body! By some strange phenomenon that he himself could not understand, he came back to life, put on an intern jacket, and escaped without anyone seeing him, walking out of the hospital. Morgues always have an escape handle inside the freezer, in case an attendant gets locked in. We don't usually have to worry about people who are in morgues getting out.

Alex makes his way back to America. Though he dies periodically when his heart stops, he always comes back to life. He keeps a medical record of his subnormal temperatures — their intervals and lengths — in a diary. But he doesn't want anyone to know that he has recovered or that he has had these experiences, because he says, "I don't want people to see me as a medical freak instead of a doctor." Neither Marie nor her husband, Alex, want to acknowledge that they have experienced any special, indescribable interventions. They both want to remain quiet about it, keep it a secret, because they are afraid it will interfere with their lives. They are fearful that this so-called vision or intervention would cause their lives to be changed.

So Marie, who couldn't deny the vision which she thought God gave to her for a purpose, never told anyone about it except two priests. Later, she met a very devout, saintly nun. This nun had dreams constantly, for years, of this same vision. So Marie carried her to the exact spot. The very pious nun experienced the same apparition. Now Marie was free, because she could say that this revelation or good news she had wasn't just hers, it was also Sister Anna's. Because Sister Anna was a pious woman, she was willing to surrender her life to that vision. Now Marie could let Sister Anna have it and forget it. Her conscience wouldn't haunt her any longer. As Marie made her way back up the hill to the motel at Big Sur to tell her husband that she was going to leave him for another man, the last words of the book say this: "She had been returned to her ordinary life, to its burdens, to its consequences, for someone else had had the vision."

God tires of us, I am sure. He tries to get through to us in many ways, to break through to us and we, like Marie and her husband, try to ward off, to deny God's intrusion. We are glad to let Jeremiah or the shepherds have an experience for us; for that kind of intrusion would make too drastic a change in our life. We sing "O come,

O come, Immanuel" but we really don't mean it!

Let's look at this biblical text for Advent. Examine Jeremiah, who had the experience and who didn't deny his vision as we probably deny many of ours. The Lord sent this vision or message to Jeremiah, while he was still in jail and Jerusalem was under siege by the great Babylonian army. This vision was about the hopes and promises of the future. The good that God would do for Judah and Israel was that He would bring to the throne, to rule with justice and peace, the "true son of David." Jeremiah, like Marie, couldn't deny his vision but hoped that God would give it to someone older.

Only thirty-six years before 622 B.C., Josiah had brought a great reformation with the "Back to the Bible" movement. But, after the big revival, everyone went back to their old wicked ways.

Now I am sure God exposed his special apparition or vision to many other persons besides Jeremiah, but he was the only one who would acknowledge and affirm this vision and message. God must surely tire of trying to get through to us! To acknowledge his revelation will change our lives, make us different from those around us. It will interrupt our lives as it did Jeremiah's. The vision was visible to all, yet only a few responded to it. The possibility of joy and hope to a world content with things as they are is never a popular message. Furthermore, it is always misinterpreted as a judgment.

For example, we have the same situation 600 years later, recorded in Luke 2:1-20. The vision that appeared to Jeremiah in the darkness of his jail cell appeared to a group of shepherds on the hillside.

In fact, Jeremiah is saying this King will bring "Shalom" which means "salvation from lostness and destruction." This means peace that comes through hope.

I. A Vision From God On High

"Glory to God in the highest." That is the first thing in a vision. Every vision, experiencing God, in the Bible was almost the same. When Isaiah had his experience in the temple, what did he see? "Holy, holy, holy is the Lord God of hosts." How did Jesus say you should pray indicating you had the experience? "Our Father who art in heaven, hallowed be thy name." You see, you have got to get right. You must begin by acknowledging that you have received a revelation from the transcendent God, the Heavenly Father.

Unless we catch that vision of glory to God in the highest, we will never find the motivation or the sustaining power to bring peace on earth and good will to all humankind. It is imperative that you experience and acknowledge the transcendent God and His revelation, not try to deny it like Marie and Alex and a thousand others. God cannot ever become imminent in your life until first of all you have experienced Him transcendentally; that you have known Him as glory to God in the highest.

If our being "human" is not the result of our relationship with God as a child of God, then we are no more important than an amoeba, a puppy dog, or a cow. It is only because we have experienced God that we then assume the goal of ourselves and our fellow human beings.

II. On Earth Peace and Good Will Toward Men

Jeremiah uses the term "Yahweh — our — Integrity," which is the symbolic messianic name for Jerusalem. Actually, the name Jerusalem means the place of Shalom or Peace. "Jeru" means "site or foundation of" and "Shalom" means "Peace" or "Peace, Good Will to Men." So Jeremiah is saying that to experience the vision he experienced from God will bring Shalom or, as we call it, peace on earth and goodwill to man "even in our immediate predicaments."

Peace on earth and good will toward all humankind can't take place unless you first experience the heavenly host. Do you understand that? You are wasting your time if you think that you can have peace on earth and good will toward all humankind, unless you have first found the one and only power who can bring that to pass.

Today we are more prepared for war than peace, aren't we? We are a lot better prepared to fight than we are to make peace. Both America's and Russia's largest industries are selling arms to other nations. As a boy, I went to see the cowboy movies on Saturdays and, if someone was caught selling arms to Indians, he was executed. We talk about serious penalties for people who sell drugs or any other kinds of killing agents to humankind. I agree that we ought to have strict punishment for drug dealing. My God, what should the world do to any of us who sell weapons to the rest of the world.? It ought to be as serious an offense as to those who sell drugs or other destructive materials. I have people say to me, "You are just an idealistic preacher. Get down to reality." You say peace isn't realistic. I tell you: you are wrong! We are living in a fantasy world if we think peace is unrealistic. If we think violence and nuclear war are realistic, we really need to be in a psychiatric ward. There is nothing realistic about that, nothing realistic about nuclear explosion. Peace is the only realistic thing there is. Nuclear explosion and war are unrealistic.

We have got to learn how to drop the Spirit of Retaliation to meet it and overcome it. We must move beyond dealing with it philosophically. Non-violence refuses to give a person a reason to hurt you, and the whole root — which is the reality of violence — surfaces and has to be faced.

Let me read to you from the diary of a young black girl who was the first one of the blacks to sit at the lunch counter in Greensboro, North Carolina, an event which made history. She writes: "A man grabbed me, twisted my arm and pushed me against the wall. It was my first experience with violence. I saw his fear and anguish in his eyes. As I thought what fear could make a man treat a defenseless girl like this, suddenly the peace of Jesus came over me. I knew for the first time violence could be taken and triumphed over." Jeremiah writes, "In those days and at that time I will cause a righteous Branch to spring forth for David; and he shall execute justice and righteousness in the land. In those days Judah will be saved and Jerusalem will dwell securely. And this is the name by which it will be called: the Lord is our righteousness."

What do we mean by peace and good will to all mankind? One Sunday while I was preaching, an eleven-year-old lad, who is an identical twin, decided, thank God, that he had something more important to do than listen to one of my sermons. He had what I call a vision. You can call it what you want — insight, inspiration, revelation — but I call it a vision. The boy composed a prayer during church and on the way home, and he read the prayer at his family's table at lunch. "Lord, thank you for the food you have blessed our lives with and thank you for the good things you have done for us. Please help . . . " Then he listed the people in the bulletin who were in the hospital. He continued, "Please help the children who are being abused and neglected. Please help us with our family relationships. Also, please help the needy families in Kenya and the hungry, poor and sick around the world." The family had passed an old beat-up wreck of a car. So he ended his prayer with this sentence: "Please help us with our reactions toward people having trouble with their cars." God has a hard time finding persons who will receive His vision and acknowledge it!

Jeremiah 33:14-15:

> *Behold, the days are coming, says the Lord, when I will fulfill the promise I made to the house of Israel and the house of Judah. In those days and at that time I will cause a righteous Branch to spring forth for David; and he shall execute justice and righteousness in the land.*

Malachi 3:1-4   *Advent 2*

Can We Pass Inspection?

Morris Wood's latest novel, *The Clowns of God,* has one specific plot. The Pope, who is a sincere, honest, pragmatic man, not given to mysticism or emotionalism, has a revelation from God that Jesus is coming right away. He feels a sense of integrity to share this announcement with the whole world that everyone might engage in the Advent, which means to prepare for His coming.

Some of the cardinals in the Vatican Council get word that he is going to make the announcement and they panic. This would upset the whole world. It is all right for military strategists, for political columnists, for economists, for the Pentagon to say that nuclear war is on the shadow of the horizon and the end is coming soon. But don't let any *religious* man say that! They realize that, if people thought that Jesus was coming soon, the institutional church would lose some of its authority and there would be a weakening of the organizational structure of the church. Gangsters, mobsters, and political dictators around the world would get word that he might make this announcement, and that would destroy all their projects for crime, all their wars and dishonest treaties and alliances. How could you get someone to go out and fight a war against his brother when he thought that tomorrow Jesus was coming? People would drop their arms and go home. In the novel, economists were frightened because, if people thought that Jesus was coming tomorrow, it would destroy the whole economic structure of the world. Who would care about material things, about the Dow Jones average, about Wall Street, if they thought that tomorrow Jesus was coming? All the "powers that be" realized that they had to do something immediately! They had to dilute the Pope's message and revelation or silence him. There were all kinds of plots, not only to dilute what he said, but to assassinate him.

We see all kinds of strategy to dilute the message of Advent, which is that Jesus is coming and you had better get ready. For example, we start celebrating Christmas at Thanksgiving. We don't have Advent any longer. Even church people don't want to sing Advent hymns. They want to sing Christmas carols in Advent. We see the same kinds of gimmicks going on in the commercial world, trying to keep us so busy and so occupied with the things and the activities of Christmas time that we don't really have time to get down and spiritually examine *ourselves* and repent. During Advent, as in Lent, the church puts up the colors of purple (or blue) on the altar to remind us we need to repent, but we go on with the green, red, and white as our Christmas colors. With our parties and our shopping we try to cover up the sins and the frailties in our lives. It is one of the gimmicks of diluting the message. Instead of cleaning up our lives and our home, what do we do? We don't dust the table. We sprinkle cotton or snow across it so we don't see the dust and we stick reindeer on top. Or we hang up tinsel and wreaths to cover the spiderwebs. We don't clean our house in the corner; we put a Christmas tree over there. If the dirt looks bad, we put some lights around to distract. We cover up with all of our decorations and activities worse than Watergate. But the ultimate reality is that there is dirt and sin in our lives.

Now let's be honest. The world would try and stop me right now from bringing to you the revelation from God which says that Jesus is coming. They would try and stop me, but they don't because they don't believe that you will believe me. Let's look at this passage.

The Gospel of Mark begins with this revelation, God-prophesied by Isaiah:

Behold, I will send a messenger, before Thy face,
Who shall prepare Thy way;
The voice of one crying in the wilderness.
Prepare the way of the Lord
Make His paths straight.

The concept of a forerunner or a messenger to get everyone ready and prepared was a part of the messianic hope of Israel during Malachi's era. John the Baptist came to take on characteristics of this "forerunner." He became the prototype of Malachi's messenger.

The purpose was to remind the children of Israel of the prerequisites for the Messiah's coming which require confession, repentance, purification and refinement of our sin. All reformation begins with moral and ethical reform which is the "getting ready" ritual. Malachi's Advent message was that we cannot fool God the way we fool ourselves and others. Just as a "refiner's fire" chemically separates pure silver and gold from other alloys, so God's coming will separate the pure in heart from those with mixed motives and morals. This prophet is calling us to clean our house and get it ready, because God will not enter or dwell in a life that is not clean.

I. Confess Sins

Malachi writes, "Who can abide?" The Bible talks about confession as "acknowledgment of." A lot of us see sin in our lives, but we don't acknowledge it as sin or identify it as sin, do we? We have our rationalizations or our interpretations or our qualifications. We don't just directly acknowledge it as sin. You could have sinful thoughts and acts existing in your life and not have the knowledge of the impact that it makes on your soul and the kind of impact that your wrong decision or action has made on God and others. Confession means not only acknowledging but admitting. But it is hard to confess our sins, isn't it? It is tough.

The reason we are not so fanatic about cleaning house is that we are not so conscious of dirt. You don't know what cleaning house is unless you saw my grandmother clean house. Twice a year, in the spring and in the fall, everything in the house had to come out — every piece of furniture: everything! All the clothing in every closet and all the junk had to come out. Can you imagine that? Twice a year all the mattresses had to be placed on horses in the yard to be aired, beaten, and cleaned. After she got everything out in the yard (that had to be done by seven a.m.) and sitting in the sunshine, she proceeded to clean the house. She had a black wash pot filled with boiling lye which she diluted a little bit with water. She had a cornshuck mop with which she scrubbed the floors, the walls, everything. The floor would be so clean that I would be scared to sit on it in the middle of August in my short pants because the lye would take the skin off my rump. And then she had this secret potion for getting rid of the possibility of bedbugs. It was camphor and turpentine. You would take a little feather and dip it in the potion and put it down in the lock where the bed fitted together. She had to take the beds apart. Everything was sterilized! Now she was conscious of a world around her that was filthy.

You and I pretend it is not that way. We cover it up with our carpets, decorations, and furniture. We hit it here and there with a vacuum cleaner or we hide the spiderwebs with a wreath. And so it is in our own lives. You and I need to confess our sins. Luther says that the moment after his confession was the cleanest and best moment of his life. Everyday when he confessed his sin he felt clean. This is the greatest moment in life, when we have confessed our sins, for only a sinner needs a Savior. Yes, we must confess. That is the first preparation.

II. Repentance

Malachi asks, "Who can stand?" The second thing Malachi told to the people of his day to do in order to get ready for the coming of Jesus was to repent. It is not enough just to confess. I know a lot of people who go around confessing their sins. "Oh, I did this." "Oh, I did that." They love to give testimony about how terrible their sins were. But that is not repentance. Repentance means to "turn around," away from the direction we are going, toward God. Isaiah called it "returning to the Lord." Jesus, in the parable of the prodigal son, described repentance when he said, "and he turned and returned to his father." That is repentance. I saw a bumper sticker last week that said, "If we are separated from God, who moved?" That is what repentance is. We turn around and go towards God. It is not just enough to confess; we have to repent of our sins.

The Bible's call to repentance means that you still have a chance to go in another direction. I heard of an old preacher who was preaching a sermon on repentance. On the pulpit he trapped a fly and pressed the fly's wing against the pulpit. He said, "The last judgment is really the final blow." And he reared back his other hand to swat the fly. As his hand came down the fly flew away. He said, "That's the way it is; there's still a chance!" He was trying to say to the congregation, "There's still a chance!" A call to repentance means there's a chance for us to go in the other direction.

Graham Greene, one of the great authors of our time, wrote a book entitled *The Heart of the Matter,* which I liked very much. It was about a fellow named Scobie who was morally better than any man I have ever heard described. He only committed a few sins in life. But his problem was he couldn't repent of the ones that he committed. There is a scene in which he is talking with the priest. The priest says to him. "It is better to sin seventy times seven and repent each time than to sin once and not repent. You can't have the end without the means!" And Scobie answered, "Oh, I'm sorry for all of them; I feel guilty for all of them, but I cannot promise to stop." Now that is the difference between confession and repentance. Confession is to admit it and feel guilty about it. Repentance is to stop, to turn around and go in another direction. You and I need that radical kind of repentance.

III. Refine and Purify

But the third and final preparation that Malachi said we must make is to be purified. We must understand that "purification" is nothing like what you and I have made it today. We have made it a sacrament, an ordinance, and we call it baptism. In the Bible, baptism and purification were spiritual acts that one daily performed to purify one's self. Every Jew baptized himself before he ate even a sandwich. They cleansed themselves. They washed using water. Before they prayed, they baptized. It was imperative. That is what Luther meant when he said, "I must be baptized daily. Every day I must be washed in the blood of Jesus, to have all my sins cleaned." That is what John the Baptist was thinking about when, out in the wilderness, he sat and watched that water, clean and pure, rushing down. Water has the ability to purify like nothing else in this universe. He says. "You must be washed; you must be baptized." I need it every day. It is a marvelous feeling.

Early every morning I run, and when I get back, I am perspiring and hot. I sit and read for about an hour and a half, until I start getting chilled and smelling so bad I can't stand myself. When it gets to that point I get up, fix a cup of hot Sanka, and go take my shower. I tell you, it must be a sin to feel that good! When you get that bath and get cleansed and clean, *that* is a good feeling! Have you ever experienced that spiritually? When you really get washed, your whole inner being cleansed, that is a marvelous feeling. That is why John said, "You must be baptized." God said to the children of Israel on Mt. Sinai the day before he made the covenant and gave them the Ten Commandments, "Back to your tents and wash, cleanse yourselves, and put on your best clothes for tomorrow. You must be cleaned and washed." Most of us need a good scrubbing to be purified, don't we?

I heard of a fellow who was being baptized. He was one of the meanest fellows in the neighborhood but had a change of heart. They were down by the river. The preacher had the man out in the water and looked up to the congregation on the bank and said, "Now, does anyone have any reason why I shouldn't baptize brother so-and-so?" An old fellow in a Western hat standing in the back shouted, "Well, no, but I just want to remind you that he has always been a mean man and just one dip won't be enough for him. What you need to do is anchor him out in the deep water overnight." That is why the Bible says you must be baptized. It is not just a once-and-for-all kind of thing. It is a daily cleansing of your life to get ready for the coming of Christ.

When my grandmother thought we were going to have company, she scrubbed me so hard the skin almost came off. We need to clean up for the coming of Jesus. In the early church, up to the eleventh century, the baptismal pools or fonts were outside of the church. They weren't inside the church buildings. They would build a little chapel outside the church for them. At the leaning tower of Pisa, Italy, there is a baptismal pool outside the church. You must go to the baptismal pool before you can go in the church. You must get baptised and cleansed before you can go into the presence of God.

You and I need that purification in our lives. We need an Advent. We need to hear Malachi's message, that revelation from God that Jesus is coming. And we need to get ready by the confession of our sins, by the repentance of our sins, and to be baptized and purified. He is coming! We need to get ready!

Zephaniah 3:14-20 *Advent 3*

His Coming is to be Welcomed, Not Feared

One of the main objectives of the Moody Institute of Religion and Science is to relate science and the holy Scripture. Several years ago, Moody produced a three-hour movie depicting the creation. It is the most marvelous film of its kind I have ever viewed. For example, it shows creation and the miracle of creation in its many stages. A seed of corn and a flower seed are implanted in the soil. A movie camera is focused on both of these seeds for four months, twenty-four hours a day, every second of the hour. At the end of four months, by the process of fast action lens. they reduced this process from four months to twenty seconds; so that before your eyes. you could view the miracle of creation. You could see that seed from the moment of its implantation in the earth, as it burst through the soil and grew into a stalk, and then as an ear of corn. You could hear the sound of the ear as it began to blossom and burst and the flower as it bloomed. I thought I had truly stood in the very presence of the Almighty as I watched it.

One problem with this film was that the fast action cameras were not able to relate or capture what took place between the implanting of the seed and the blossoming of the flower. It showed nothing that the horticulturist or the farmer must have done, nothing of the tilling of the soil, nothing of having to fertilize it, weed it, or water it. As I reflected on the film, I realized that while I had seen a fragment of the miracle of creation, I had only seen a part. For I had not seen that which took place from the beginning to the end in terms of cultivation.

Now, Advent is to teach us the art of what we do between the implantation and the coming of Christ. It is to teach us what goes on during that interval. It is to teach us how to wait creatively, and to know what takes place between the beginning and the end, between the eschaton and the coming of Christ eschalogically, what we do between the promise and the fulfillment. Advent is to teach us how to practice waiting creatively and how to use our time constructively and creatively.

Zephaniah is saying that the seed has already been implanted in the earth . . . the eschaton and the Lord's coming has already been decided. We are in the interval period between the seed having been planted and the blossoming of the rose of Sharon. We need to use creatively this period of waiting . . . to wait patiently and creatively, by being busy rejoicing, and to "let not your hands grow weak." (verse sixteen) But most of all, Zephaniah is saying his coming is not to be feared but looked forward to . . . that his judgment is not to damn us but to disperse justice and make all things right, and to "remove disaster from you". (verse eighteen)

I. The Lord is Coming

That is the message of Advent. He came once in Bethlehem and He will come again. In any intellectual circle, that is the proof for the fact that anything is going to happen. In a court of law, for example, proof is tied to precedent. In the field of science you say, "Well, because this sequence occurred one time, then it will occur again, that is the proof." The historian ties proof to the principle that history repeats itself. The Bible uses this same argument: because Jesus came once, He *will* come again.

For God, there is no such thing as time. The end and the beginning are the same, but he can view the world and life from eternity reaching to the future to the present, and from the present reaching back to the past. In other words, God sees it all, but you and I stand back here looking from the perspective of the past toward the future.

Yes, He is coming! We don't know when or exactly how. Jesus said, "You know not the day nor hour when the Son of Man comes." The disciples said, "Lord, give us some signs so we will know when you are coming, whether in a few weeks or years." But He said, "No, you wicked generation. a sign will not be given you."

In fact, the New Testament says the way you can tell a false prophet is: "A false prophet will always give you the impression that he has got some special insight or understanding about when Jesus will come." Always, the Bible says you can tell they are false prophets if they say they know when Jesus will come. Some passages suggest that He will come instantaneously, like a flash in the night or a call in the middle of the night. Others say He will come quietly and slowly, like the yeast in the dough or the small mustard seed that is planted, sprouts out and grows up into a huge tree. Some say it will be like the description in "O Little Town of Bethlehem," where we sing:

> *How silently, how silently*
> *The wondrous gift is given*
> *So God imparts to human heart*
> *The blessings of his heaven.*
> *No ear may hear his coming,*
> *But in this world of sin.*
> *Where meek souls will receive him still,*
> *The dear Christ enters in.*

Others say it will be a physical return. Still others say it will be a spiritual return. The Bible says both. It says, in John's gospel, "and the word became flesh" (that is physical) and dwelt among us and he will come in like manner again. And there are other passages that indicate to us that it will be a spiritual coming. For Jesus said, "I won't leave you alone forever, I will come again and receive you unto myself. My spirit shall come and be in you. The world doesn't see me, but you see me because in my spirit I live and dwell within you." No, we don't know how or when, but we do know He is coming. It will be a combination of the physical and spiritual. It will be a combination between the slow and the gradual and the instantaneous, but He will come!

II. *Learn to be Patient*

This scripture from Zephaniah teaches us that we need to learn how to be patient. Most of us lack the virtue of patience. If you are like me, you pray, "Lord, make me patient, but not right now. I ain't got time." We are instant-minded — instant coffee, instant food service, instant pizza, instant TV, instant hot water, instant everything. If God doesn't respond right away. we say "forget it, Mac, you ain't listening." That is just the way we react. We forget that God has an eternity and he isn't in any hurry. He has all the time of the world at his disposal.

I am impatient. During Advent we sing the Advent Christmas carols. I had rather sing "O Little Town of Bethlehem" and "Joy to the World." I can't wait for Christmas. I am impatient. I am worse than the children. I can't wait until Christmas to sing "Joy to the world, the Lord has come."

We need to be patient like the farmer. Most of us say farmers don't have anything to do, they just plant the seed and between gathering it in, they hunt, fish. and play golf. But you farmers know better than that. There are many things you have to do in between: cultivate the soil, weed it, fertilize it, water it and irrigate it. That is what Zephaniah is saying you and I are supposed to be doing: taking the example of the farmer, staying busy cultivating the kingdom of God while we are waiting for the coming of Jesus. The Bible says, "What you do from the time the seed is planted to the time of His coming is the performance upon which you are going to be judged. We shall be judged by that." In fact, Jesus said, "Blessed is he who, when his master comes, find him so doing."

Do you remember the parable of the talents? Talents were given to two fellows, and they got busy until the master came and put them to work. But one fellow took his talent and said, "The Lord is coming any day. I will wait for His coming." That is all he did. So when the Lord came, He found him not doing anything but waiting, and he threw him out.

The early Christians began to think (they misunderstood Jesus' sayings) that the end was coming any day. So, they quit working. We read in the Acts of the Apostles that they quit their jobs, stopped planting their seeds, sold their homes, gave away their possessions and generally tried to disregard the earthly life. Paul encouraged them to do that in 1 Corinthians but later Paul began to understand what Jesus really was saying. That is why Paul wrote in 2 Corinthians that he had been wrong. We are not supposed to just quit. We are supposed to be like a farmer, and cultivate while we are waiting.

For instance, it is sometimes hard to get millennium and second-coming kinds of Christians to work in a church or do the Lord's work. They think he is coming any day so they just wait, because he is going to make all things right. Yet it says in James, "By what you do during that interval, by that you shall be judged."

Have you ever considered that if Paul and the early Christians had not changed their point of view, that Jesus was likely coming any second, we would not have the New Testament? Prior to that they didn't write anything down. They didn't need to. Jesus was coming any day (they thought). In fact, the early written Scriptures say, "and thus you have heard it has been said," but later on they say, "and thus it has been written." When they realized they were supposed to be about God's work in the interval time, they began to write the Scripture down and record it for us.

Reflect on the parable of the ten virgins; five were wise and five were foolish. The foolish did what? From the time of the announcement of the wedding to the time of the coming of the bridegroom, they lost their souls because they didn't do anything in the interval. We need to learn how to be patient.

When I counsel people, no matter what their problem, I find myself almost always doing the same thing. A young wife comes in. Her husband has left her. She is depressed. After we have gone through the whole listening process, I end by saying: "You are grieving yourself to death. You are depressed and you are making yourself sick. What God is going to make you answer for is what you are doing during this period of waiting." You think, "I hope maybe we can get back together, or I hope something will work out." "Wait a minute," I say, "you can't do anything about him. I can't either. But you can do something about *you!* And that is what God is going to judge you for. Now what I want you to do during this interval time of waiting is to be certain not to waste your time. I want you to work at making yourself more beautiful. I want you to become the most beautiful girl in town. I want you to concentrate on your spiritual life, to read the word of God every day and to pray. I want you to get involved in service to others. I want you to do some things that you can accomplish and achieve, so that you will feel good about yourself and love yourself and know you are beautiful because you have let God make you beautiful. So if it *does* turn out that there is a possibility of reconciliation somewhere down the line, or that you must start over, you will be a beautiful person to start a new life."

For someone in this position, I usually ask them, "Wait a minute. Let's say that what you want for you and your husband is to be reconciled right now, but what would you have? You would have the same thing you had to start with, and worse. You have told me he hasn't grown spiritually while you have been separated and you tell me all you have been doing while you have been separated is grieving and that you haven't grown spiritually. So you would have a bad marriage. You need to use this time to make yourself beautiful." Yes, we need to learn how to fill that interval period and how to be patient.

III. The Lord Has Taken Away The Judgments Against You.

Zephaniah says, "The Lord has taken away the judgment against you." (verse fifteen) "Also, I will change their shame into praise." (verse nineteen) When in verse twenty he says, "I will restore your fortune," Zephaniah is saying the Lord comes not to condemn the world but that the world might be saved.

After the movie, "The Day After", a scientist said to me, "We scientists have now looked in the mouth of hell and we are afraid, preacher." I replied, "For centuries, we ministers have been dealing with the deep and dark problems of humankind. We have looked into the mouth of hell and we are not afraid."

There is nothing about which we should be frightened, or should dread, concerning the judgment. I can't wait! That is the thing to which I look forward. That is the thing for which every Christian can live with hope. He is going to come and judge the world but, through the "suffering servant," he takes on himself my sin and iniquity. All wrong is going to be made right. I don't have to worry about a thing. I am a horrible sinner and am far from perfect. But I am going to point to Jesus when He says, "Now I need to examine you," and I will say, "There, examine *him,*" and I am going to be saved by *his* works, not mine. I have trusted in Jesus and him alone and I don't have to worry about a thing. He will pass the judgment.

My father-in-law used to be a great fox hunter. He had the best dogs in the state, about four packs. He could identify the hound with the tenor voice, soprano or contralto, and call them by name. It was beautiful music. He could tell by the sound of their voice whether they were chasing a gray fox or a red one. These dogs get incredibly excited when they get on the path of a red one. Red foxes are smarter than gray ones. I remember a time when we chased a red fox all night. We turned out four fresh packs of hounds, but I knew they wouldn't catch that red fox. About dawn, I was out in the woods trying to find some of the dogs and, looking up on the side of a cliff, I saw this beautiful red fox stretching out on the edge of the cliff licking his paw. The hounds were scrambling down below unable to climb that rock. They were baying and barking and the fox didn't pay them any attention. You see, he was in his refuge. He had gone to his den, where he knew he was protected from all things. All the baying and barking of the hounds didn't upset him or frighten him. He wasn't afraid of the judgment at all, for he was secure.

That is what the Bible teaches. You and I are supposed to *look forward* to the judgment, because we know we have our refuge in Jesus. He is our Savior and we can look down on all the baying of the hounds and all the problems of life in the world and know we are protected. Be patient and wait upon the coming of the Lord, for he is coming. Because I trust Jesus, I will not fear the judgment.

Glory hallelujah, jubilee. I can't wait! Can you?

Micah 5:2-5a   Advent 4

The Happy Hour

There is nothing lonelier than standing on the railroad track in a small town waiting for a train to come from somewhere in the distance. Even in flat country, you can always hear the train before you can see it. There is something about the conduit of the tracks carrying the sound. On a dark, cloudy, dreary day, I stood at a barren crossroads with a middle-aged man, waiting for a train to bring the coffin containing the body of his oldest son who had been killed in Vietnam. We didn't say much. We were the only people there. I knew what kind of hopes he had had for that boy. We didn't talk, but just stood there and looked down the tracks. The mother, sisters and wife of the young man sat silently in the car. The widow of the young man was three months pregnant. We wondered whether or not she would lose the child. Her life seemed to have come to an end. The family had almost lost hope.

Only the hope of that conception and what it could materialize into gave the widow a little strength to continue. She did give birth. That hope had been enough to keep her going. Suddenly, not only to her, but to the rest of that family came anticipation. Once they held that child in their arms, once they looked into his face, they saw that that for which they had hoped would be realized. They saw the future for her in her son. They saw a remnant. They saw hope. But more than that, they began once again to anticipate.

Micah was a contemporary of Isaiah. His messages give evidence that he was familiar with Isaiah and expresses the same concerns, philosophy, and hope. The children of Israel had been through twenty bad kings of Judah since David. With each, they had hoped idealistically for a good king, only to be disappointed. They had just been completely ravaged by the Assyrian Army. Their homes had been burned, city walls torn down, and the temple destroyed. Their sons had been killed, leaving no one to carry on the family name and removing any hope or chance for continuation. There was no tomorrow! Sitting on the ash heaps, covered with soot and smoke from the smouldering homes and burned dreams, one of their hometown boys named Micah came sharing hope. He said, "From Bethlehem shall come forth a King whose origin is from of old, from ancient of days." (Micah 5:2) Now they had seen many kings crowned and anointed, and all of them had become corrupt and failed. But Micah is saying of this one:

And he shall stand and feed his flock,
in the strength of the Lord,
And they shall dwell secure, for now
he shall be great to ends of the earth.

I. Hope — Micah 5

"The exiles, remnants of Israel, will rejoin their brethren in their own land." Micah says "conception" has taken place, and "it is only a matter of time." He is saying there is hope. Micah is saying, I don't care how bad your situation is or how sad it might be. I don't care what are the blows of life that might have been dealt you — how many times your home is burned and pillaged, how you are beaten, your teeth kicked out, your pride and your hope gone. Although you have been brutalized and life has trampled you and you are sitting in the smouldering ashes of all your dreams and ideals, you still do not give up hope. Hope is the conception, and that conception has taken place. Though there are the nine long months of waiting and the pain of birth awaits, conception keeps you with hope. Micah is saying that conception already has taken place in the mind, the providence, and the plan of God. You are pregnant, swelling with possibilities.

I saw this young mother whose husband was killed in war, and as she went through the sorrow and grief, I saw out of that grief come hope. Suddenly she became large enough to put on a maternity smock and that life began to move within her and hope once again sprang forth. You and I read Micah as if it was a description of praise where it says, "Unto us a Child is given." We think, "Praise God, He gave Jesus." But you must remember and understand they were hearing it before the fact. It was not a description of praise to them; it was the promise or the possibility of something yet to come . . . hope.

One of my favorite stories comes from late 18th century in Poland, when the Kaiser's forces were burning all the Jewish villages. They had burned one particular village to the ground and exploited everyone within the reach of their swords. The town smelled of hot blood and the fumes of smouldering ashes. As the sun came up the next morning one old Jew went down to the marketplace and got in his stall and opened it for business. One of the young men said, "Old Jew, what are you selling?" Standing there in the smouldering remains he said, "I am selling hope." You can sell water on a dry desert, so the place to sell hope is on the ash heap of destruction. Hope — "Unto us a child is given."

Every time a rescue takes place, when someone has been out in the ocean or in a well or cave or stranded in the jungle for a long time, when they are interviewed by the press they are inevitably asked, "Well, what was it that kept you alive?" And what do they say? "I never gave up." Sometimes I would like to call all those that died and did not make it back from death and ask, "Why was it you did not make it?" I am sure you know what they would have to say.

"Unto us a child is born." Conception has taken place. You can look in the face of a pregnant mother and see a glow, a beauty, and excitement that is not there normally. There is the promise of what conception can bring. There is the expectancy of it all. "Unto us a child is given."

II. Anticipation — Micah 5:4

But then after the birth there comes the anticipation. It didn't just end with hope, but once you hold a child you begin to anticipate what the child will become. "And he shall stand and feed his flock in the strength of the Lord, in the majesty of the name of the Lord his God. And they shall dwell secure, for now he shall be great to the ends of the earth." Mothers begin to dream what their sons and daughters will become and then follows anticipation. I do not like to be around people who do not anticipate. I have to confess I am prejudiced. I guess that is why I enjoy being around children more than most adults because they anticipate. Christmas to them seems like a million years away, like it will never get here. They anticipate bicycles, ice cream cones and "cotton patch dolls." They live with a sense of anticipation. That is why Advent is my favorite time of the year, because most of us older people can at this season even anticipate a little bit. We look forward to the possibilities of certain things. I like people who anticipate miracles, fulfillment of dreams and hopes.

The Old Testament says that everyone before the coming of Jesus was supposed to face life that way. This is what 50% of the Old Testament is about. It is saying that you are supposed to face life standing on your tiptoes with the rapture of a forward look — with expectancy. The worse the situation, the more you ought to expect. Sometimes I think maybe the anticipation is as valuable as the thing we anticipate.

Some of the most emotional moments for me are when I go every year to the baccalaureate and graduation ceremonies and see some of the fathers and mothers of those children graduating. The son brings his dad up to meet the college president or you the speaker. He introduces you and the dad uses grammar like "You was" instead of "You were", and the son is a little embarrassed. And you want to say to him when you see the tears in the father's eyes, "Son, there are things you will learn that are more important than saying, 'You were.' " And you look out there and see those tearstained faces of mothers and fathers who are so excited that their son or daughter is walking across the stage. It is the fulfillment of their hopes and dreams. They have anticipated what he or she will become, and they are seeing it realized.

A man stood on the George Washington Bridge preparing to jump off. Thousands of people gathered, including the firemen and police. A priest tried to talk him down without success. Finally a fellow by the name of Homer Wright went up and got out on the ledge with the man and said, "Listen, I know what trouble is. I have plenty of it. I have a seven-year-old boy who has a heart defect, and has never been able to walk or play like other children. I pass this bridge every day and I have thought many times of jumping off. Next year my son is supposed to have an operation. Maybe it will work. Maybe it will not. But things can get better. You have to have hope." A few minutes later they climbed down the bridge together and, as the man was taken to the hospital, they interviewed Homer and asked him what he said to the man. Homer said, "Well, I felt for the guy. He's got trouble. I've got trouble, too, but a man's got to stay with it." That is what hope is about.

I used to not be able to understand why the people in the Third World countries had so many children until I talked with some of them. The average man in India figures he wants to have at least fifteen children, because he figures that, if he has fifteen, maybe seven or eight of them will survive. Of those eight, maybe four of them will be male. And of those four, maybe two of them will outlive him. And of those two, maybe one of them will be prosperous enough to take care of him in his old age. He doesn't have Social Security; he doesn't have old age pensions; he doesn't have Medicare and Medicaid. The only thing he's got is fifteen children . . . the only hope he has of any kind of dignity or anyone caring for him in his old age. The only hope for a man like Abraham who is past childbearing age is for a son. And you and I know how important that is. When we anticipate, the Father tries to answer our anticipation. You earthly fathers, if your child anticipates an ice cream cone, you end up buying an ice cream cone. don't you? Or if the child anticipates one day being big enough to have a bicycle, you try your best to get him a bicycle.

When I was in seminary I had three small children, and they were anticipating Christmas and a tree. We didn't even have any lights. We found some old lights up at the church but didn't have a tree. When I was a boy we went out in the woods and cut a tree. We didn't go pay $50 for one at the store because we didn't have $50. As I drove back and forth to Divinity School everyday with three other guys, I spotted a lot of big cedar trees on Highway 70 between Raleigh and Durham. They were thirty or forty feet high, and the top of those trees looked like they would make beautiful Christmas trees. I figured that cutting the top wouldn't do any harm, because the wood would still be there.

So I took a saw with me to school one day, and, on the way home, stopped on the side of the road. I told the fellows I was going to get myself a Christmas tree and to wait in the car and watch for me. I climbed up to the top of this great big cedar with coat and tie still on and was sawing the top out. I was about ready to holler "Timber" when a state patrolman pulled up right down below me. I was hanging over him. All I could do was try to hold the tree in hopes that it would not fall on him. My friends in the car, wanting to tease me, held that patrolman there an extra ten minutes asking him all kinds of ridiculous questions, questions like, "Who is the Governor of North Carolina?" He finally drove away and I got that tree home. A father will do anything to fulfill the anticipation of a child. Why should you think that your Heavenly Father would not want to fulfill all your anticipation as His child? It says that they began to anticipate again that they would have a King and that "He shall be great to the ends of the earth."

One of the most beautiful stories in literature is the French classic, *The Little Prince*. There are two lines that have an Advent and Christmas message in them. The fox says to the Little Prince at one point, "If you come at four o'clock, I shall begin to be happy at three o'clock." This is the story of Advent. That is also where the expression, "The Happy Hour" came from, not from sixty minutes in which to get intoxicated before dinner. It is the happy hour of waiting. "If you come at four o'clock, I shall begin to be happy at three o'clock." That is what Advent is about, when you know that Christ is coming and you can go on and start getting happy with dreams of what he can be and do and become.

> *And he shall stand and feed his flock in the*
> *strength of the Lord, in the majesty of the*
> *name of the Lord his God.*
> *And they shall dwell secure, for now*
> *He shall be great*
> *to the ends of the earth.*

That is the message to everyone who is depressed, beaten, old, set in his ways, given up, senile, everyone of us who has failed, whose dreams have been burned up. That is the message. Conception has taken place. It is just a matter of time. That makes it "the Happy Hour."

Isaiah 52:7-10　　　　　　　　　　Christmas Eve/Christmas Day

Is There Any Word From God?

A young boy stationed in Vietnam wrote home, several years ago, these words:

> Today I am not very proud of myself. We were supposed to evacuate all the villages in a fifty mile area. Since time was a factor, we were told to waste all the livestock and waste the ones who will not move. As we went on the sweep, my buddy and I stopped at a little clay hut. Having called "La Dai" before we did it, which means "come out", we pulled the pin from the grenade and threw it into the hut. We fell to the ground and lay flat on our stomachs, waiting for the explosion. During that interval when we could only hear the fuse of the grenade spewing, we suddenly heard the cry of an infant child coming from the hut. It seemed like an eternity as I lay there, the grenade spewing, an infant child crying, and I was wondering what I should do and what was my responsibility."

Somehow all of us live in that kind of a period, the period you might call "the lapse" — that moment somewhere in between the inevitable destruction of the world which has begun . . . between the pulling of the detonators and the bang. We live somewhere in *the lapse*, where all we hear is the spewing penetrated by the sound of an infant babe's cry before the explosion. We acknowledge that we do live in this lapse of time. Global peace hangs on the threat of nuclear war. The bomb has already been made, the time clock set, the detonators of the population explosion already pulled. The world has created more persons than it can house or feed. We hear the spewing of the pollution coming out into the air. It's hard for us to appreciate how our world is being polluted to the point that hundreds die of asphxiation every day. We live in that era, where you can hear the clock ticking down, and sense the explosion is near.

We live in these days of economic crisis, days in which the world faces hunger worse than any period in history, where the rich get richer and the poor get poorer. It is a fact in our world. Not long ago, at two wedding receptions and a banquet, I ate more food than I used to eat in a week when I was a boy. We have pulled the pin on the grenade and it is spewing, and we find ourselves flat on our faces waiting. You can look into the face of the President of the United States, and see that is the position in which he finds himself . . . flat on his face, hugging the ground. not knowing what to do. He knows that the grenade pin has been pulled, but he doesn't know whether there is time enough to save the world — or even if there *is* a way. He doesn't know what to do. And you can look around you and see no signs of anyone with the answer.

Several years ago, I had dinner with the Dean of the Divinity School at Yale and the Dean of the Berkeley School of Theology. Both of these deans affirmed, as they looked out over the world and the theological religious scene, that they saw no words of hope, that they saw no new voice, no rising prophet, no new theological perspectives. Is there any message from God?

We look in the scientific world and we see the same vacuum. There are no scientists who seem to have the answer to the energy crisis, to starvation. or to pollution. We live in an age of voidness. There is a voidness in politics. What great statesman appears to have the answer? I look at both the Republican Party and the Democratic Party, and I wonder from where will we find a candidate that either party can run, one who has some of the answers to the needs of this world? No wonder Dr. Peter's book, *The Peter Principle,* says that in America sooner or later everyone will rise to his level of incompetence. By that he means that if you are a good public school teacher, they will reward you by promoting you to a principal or a supervisor or a superintendent. But a good teacher might not be a wise administrator or supervisor. This is true of industry. You might be a great salesman and they may make you president of the company, but you might be a lousy president. This is what the author means in saying that sooner or later every person will rise to his or her level of incompetence. We are breeding mediocrity. We find ourselves like those two soldiers, the grenade having been thrown, the pin pulled. and the explosion about to detonate, as we lie flat on our bellies, with our face in the mud, not knowing what to do but wait for the explosion. Lots of us find ourselves like "the old woman who lived in a shoe, who had so many children she didn't know what to do. So she gave them some broth without any bread; she whipped them all soundly and put them to bed." And that is about all we have done. We ought to realize that we live somewhere in that lapse of time. Is there no message from God, no initiative on his part?

But there is one hope! And the hope is that from the time that the detonator has been pulled, before the explosion and the end of time, that you and I, at Christmas time, might hear the cry of a newborn babe. That is the hope of the world! Lying prostrate on our stomachs waiting for the explosion in our helplessness, we might hear the cry of a newborn babe. For that is our hope!

The problem with us moderns is that we have lost our faith in miracles. We think that, because a situation looks impossible, there then is no hope. But that is what Christmas is all about. It is the affirmation that a miracle is possible, that in the midst of our turmoil and badness, the Lord might return! There is a message from God. Let us hear it.

Isaiah 52:7-10:

> *How beautiful upon the mountains*
> *are the feet of him who brings*
> *good tidings,*
> *who publishes peace, who brings*
> *good tidings of good*
> *who publishes salvation,*
> *who says to Zion, "Your God reigns."*
> *Hark, your watchmen lift up their*
> *voice,*
> *together, they sing for joy;*
> *for eye to eye they see*
> *the return of the Lord to Zion.*
> *Break forth together into singing,*
> *your waste places of Jerusalem;*
> *for the Lord has comforted his people,*
> *he has redeemed Jerusalem.*
> *The Lord has bared his holy arm*
> *before the eyes of all nations;*
> *and all the ends of the earth shall*
> *see the salvation of our God.*

Second Isaiah was a rare individual, a prophet who lived in the lapse between the Babylonian invasion and capture, and the freedom granted later under the Persians who conquered the Babylonians. It was a terrible time. Everything seemed to go from bad to worse. Nebuchadnezzar, their strong enemy seemed to be undefeatable. He put down Jehozakim. Next Zehoiachim was put in chains and taken prisoner. Then Zedekiah was blinded and shipped off to Babylon and his sons put to death. Jerusalem was ashes, and the temple burned to the ground. The royal line of David had come to an end. During this lapse Second Isaiah is the only prophetic voice which could meet the crisis with faith and hope. While he had, like First Isaiah, a deep sense of the divine providence at work in history, he also had a unique vision of the glory and possibilities of their future. Though destruction seems inevitable, though the fuse has been pulled and the world waits for the big bang, Second Isaiah says in 52:7-10 that God will intervene in time; he will defuse the enemy and God will reign and bring peace, beauty and joy. He will restore Jerusalem, and God will become visible (bare his holy arm) and all shall see his salvation. This means He will make himself known or, as Wesley wrote in his hymn, "Veiled in flesh the Godhead see".

The passage in Isaiah 52:7-10 has been referred to by scholars of Deutero-Isaiah as the angelic proclamation of the nativity. It is the proclamation of good tidings, proclaiming salvation and announcing the birth of God's King.

Israel had given up hope that God would come in time, that it was not too late. Who would have thought that, 2,500 years later, the world would sing, "Yet in the dark streets shineth, The everlasting Light; The hopes and fears of all the years, Are met in thee tonight"? This is the miracle of Christmas that in a newborn child the hopes of humanity and the plans of God are embodied.

Long ago, who would have thought that the slave girl who put that little Hebrew infant named Moses in a floating cradle and set it going down the Nile River would change the world? If you had walked down by Nolans Creek, in what's now Kentucky, and you had heard, from a one-roomed log cabin with a dirt floor, the cry of a newborn infant, you wouldn't have thought that from that log cabin, Abraham Lincoln would have been born. Or consider the humble beginnings of Charles Darwin, William Gladstone, Alfred Lord Tennyson, Edgar Allan Poe, Oliver Wendell Holmes, Cyrus

McCormack, or the great musician Mendelssohn. Who would ever have thought that in a newborn child there would be hope for the world?

Every time I read in the paper in the morning about the incidents where a child has died from a grenade or a bomb or starved to death in Bangladesh or Ethiopia or Haiti or India, I wonder, "Lord, was that the Messiah?" Possibly could that have been God become human again?

A few years ago, in a couples class in one of my congregations, a quiet man stood up and interrupted the teacher. It was the first Sunday in Advent, and the tears were streaming down his cheeks. He said, "I must tell you all something that I have never told a living soul." He put his hands on his wife's shoulder and he said, "I haven't even told my wife. When I was stationed in Germany in the second World War, we took a little village. We didn't have time to check out everything before dark, so we built a barricade with sandbags in the center of the city square. I was on guard duty during the night. We were told not to allow anyone who didn't have the password to pass." He went on, "Somewhere in the wee hours of the morning I heard sounds on the cobble streets and I cried, "Who goes there? What is the password?" No sound came, and so I cocked my machine gun and I fired at the sounds. The following morning as the sun began to peak, I looked over the barricade and saw lying on that cobble street the body of a grandmother with a newborn infant in her arms." And he said, "That has been on my soul ever since. I haven't slept well a night since then. Maybe that child might have been the Promised One. He might have been God become man."

What was it Wordsworth said? "Heaven lies all about us in our infancy." And the answer of God is found in a little child. What is our responsibility, living in this lapse of time, this voidness when, all of a sudden before the explosion, we hear the cry of an infant?

The title of this chapter started out to be, "How to Build a Manger." That is our responsibility: to build a manger. A manger is whatever may hold the Promised One. This is what Isaiah 52:7-10 is talking about. To build something in our lives and in our world and in our church and hearts that could be used to hold that newborn babe is our responsibility in Advent, to construct a life that can hold Him.

What if Herod had succeeded in destroying every infant Hebrew child? We would not have had Jesus. What if the world by starvation and war destroys all the children? Who knows what child might be the Promised One? I have a custom in my ministry of always going to the hospital when a new babe has been born and having a prayer for the new child. Last year I was in the hospital room when the young mother was preparing to take her firstborn child home. She was excited and also frightened. The hospital didn't allow parents to hold the child until they got ready to take him home. But there she was with the new baby lying on the foot of her bed. The grandmother had finished dressing the child. And you know the clothes you buy for a babe before arrival are always two sizes too big. The little baby was lost in that new suit. The mother was getting ready to take him home. Nervously she sat waiting on the bed in her new robe and bedroom shoes. I said to her, "May we have a prayer for your new baby and thank God for this great joy?" She looked at me and she looked at her baby whom she was trying to get up enough courage to hold for the first time. Suddenly she clumsily took the little baby and put him in my hands. There I stood holding that precious child in my hands. I was so overwhelmed that she had trusted him to my hands that I could hardly speak. She had entrusted to me the most precious thing that she possessed! The hopes and dreams of her whole life and body and being, I held in my hands. What a responsibility.

Now, that's what Christmas is all about. God came to us by becoming human as an infant child. What a thought, that in my and your hands we hold the hope of the world: God become human. God gives to you and me this new child, the hope of the world, and the question is, "What will you and I do with Him? The Lord has bared his holy arm before the eyes of all nations.

> *How beautiful upon the mountains are the feet of him who brings good tidings, who publishes peace, who brings good tidings of good, who publishes salvation, who says to Zion, "Your God Reigns." (Isaiah 52:7)*

1 Samuel 2:18-20, 26 *Christmas 1 (Common, Lutheran)*
Holy Family (Roman Catholic)

Spiritual Growth

The giant steel doors swung shut and the doctor put his big key in the lock. The door was to keep people from coming inside the psychiatric ward, but it was also to keep those who were inside from getting out. A giant of a man, 245 pounds, six foot five inches, came dashing towards the doctor like some ballet dancer. Spinning up on his toes, he did a beautiful ballet butterfly twirl and in the process he dropped his baby rattle. The rattle went skidding across the waxed floor. The new doctor reached down to pick up the rattle to return it to the patient, but immediately the giant reared back and took a huge swipe at the doctor, knocking him all the way across the hall and against the wall. Then, the patient went to retrieve his rattler. As I was helping the young doctor to his feet, he looked at me with bafflement and astonishment and said, "Eh gad, the body of a giant but the mind of a child."

How often you and I see that same kind of situation about us! We see people who, though they may be five foot two with eyes of blue and wear highheels, are still just a child. Or we may see men six foot two, 190 pounds and still a child. We see people fifteen and thirty-five and sixty-five years old who have all the outward appearances of an adult but they are still just children. Immature, they pout when they do not get their way. They stomp their feet or they slam doors. They may not still suck their thumbs, but they have not quite grown out of some of these other things. They always have a way of bringing the conversation back to themselves. No matter what you talk about, they bring it back to what *they* want to talk about. Like a little child, they still believe they are the center of the universe. You see these characteristics in the bigoted man of forty or the giddish woman of thirty-five who still dresses like a fifteen year old. They have not grown into maturity.

"Now the boy Samuel continued to grow both in stature and in favor with the Lord and with men." I was "stuck" trying to write this Christmas message from 1 Samuel 2:18-20, 26. Desperate for some special insight, sure that there was some novel or innovative lesson hidden in exegeting this text, I called a friend who is the Rabbi at our local synagogue. He chided me, saying, "You Christians try to read too much into the Bible instead of taking the story simply for what it is." This passage is simply about a family who received a son for whom they had waited, hoped and prayed. Out of gratitude these spiritually-minded parents dedicated Samuel to God. Because of a strong faith, they believed God could do more with their son than they. Samuel succeeded Eli because he was more dedicated and morally mature.

Growing in stature is normal for a child, but to continue to grow in favor with God and man is the result of spiritual growth and cultivation. It is a matter of love and will. All of us must continue to grow and change spiritually as we grow and change physically, if we are to reach Christian maturity.

I. Samuel Grew

How did Samuel become the mature and great man that he became? One of the main reasons so many of us do not grow spiritually any more than we do is that we get too rigid in the process of our growth. I was walking down the beach not long ago, thinking about my spiritual progress and my lack of progress. It was a sort of painful experience, to admit that I really was not making the kind of spiritual progress in my life that I ought to be making. As I walked I saw a dead crab in his shell, having been washed up on the beach by the storm. Suddenly, I remembered what I had learned in my zoology classes, that crabs will live on and on as long as they are constantly able to discard their shell and leave it to form another one. But, the problem is that in their over-conscientiousness to create a shell that is secure, hard and protective, they will create a shell that is too rigid. They finally create one so tough that they can't discard it and so they die.

Now a lot of us have done that in our lives. We have created beliefs, philosophies, principles, and dogmas, and they get too rigid to protect our shallow faith, so that we are unable to discard them and get free and be open to the leading of the Spirit. I realized then that my lack of spiritual growth was due partly to the fact that I had become trapped and restricted by the hard shell of my beliefs and dogmas. I realized that I was, therefore, not open to the leading of the Spirit. What you and I need to do is to find security, not in our beliefs or dogmas, but in God. We make a terrible error when our security and trust is in our theological dogmas or beliefs. We are supposed to lift our eyes, not to theological principles, but to God. Our faith and security is supposed to be in him, not in our beliefs.

There was much about Bishop Pike with which I disagreed, but there was one thing that he said that we must know is true: "What Christianity needs is less beliefs and more belief." We need to be able to be free to move with the Spirit and the calling . . . to constantly change our lives. That day as I walked the beach, it hit me right in the face that one of the worst errors I was making was to assume, perhaps like all preachers before me, that the call to preach was a once-and-for-all affair. If I assume God's call to me "to preach" is forever, then I am saying that I have a closed mind and ear to his voices. God might call me to be a missionary somewhere else or to do something else. And, if I were to be free in the Spirit, free to listen to his call, I must not decide that anything is once-and-for-all, that I must surrender my life to his calling, not to a call.

One of my favorite writers is the Russian Nobel Peace winner who has written a book about the cruelty and the tragedies in the Russian concentration camps. He spent over eight years in that kind of pain and existence. In his book, *The First Circle,* he writes that "what mattered most in life was not successes or failures, but growth." He wrote, "The few of us that survived the concentration camp, we grew within our failures, and . . . success was of no value if I did not grow in the process". Oh, how we cover our own lives with hard shells of beliefs, philosophies, ideas and prejudices, so hard that we are not open to the moving of the spirit! We just do not quite "hang loose" enough. As I walked down the beach that day, I noticed a pier. It was about three years old, with pilings that looked almost new. But, someone had forgotten to clean the barnacles off them. Here was an almost new pier, that was hanging suspended in the air, because the barnacles had formed on those poles and they had cut the pole in two. Now that is what happens to the support of your whole Christian faith if you let the barnacles of rigid ideas and preconceived conceptions form and you do not scrape them off. They finally encase your life and eat all the way through until the foundations give way. What kind of cage or shell or rigid form is your life trapped and stinted in?

"He grew."

II. He Continued to Grow

We must continue growing. In other words, we cannot stop when we get into the kingdom or at the point of conversion. We must continue to grow. Paul wrote, "I press on, on towards the perfection which is in Christ Jesus." I remember that when I was thirteen, my grandfather sent me to the crossroads store, some two and a half miles away. For the first time in my life, he had trusted me with a brand new two-horse wagon with a pair of strong mules under the hood. In the hands of a teenager, two mules can be as explosive a device as a 400 horse-power engine. I sat up on that big seat on the front of the wagon like I was John Wayne personified. On the way to the store, I passed Lulie, one of the little boys who lived on my grandfather's place. Lulie was on his way to town to buy some "B-B bats." I stopped and, with an air of sophistication, said, "Lulie, would you like a ride?" "Yep," said Lulie. With a John Wayne air, I said, "Well, climb up here on the seat with me." But, Lulie preferred to jump on the tailgate and dangle his feet out back. "Ready?" I cried. "Ready," said Lulie. I pulled off the emergency brakes, showered down on the reins and away we went. But, in the process, Lulie was slung out in a mud puddle. I stopped the mules and went back to see if Lulie was all right. Pulling him up out of the mud I asked, "What happened?" He smiled with a real big grin and said, "Well, I guess I sat too close to where I got in."

Now often this is a problem with many of us. We sit too close to where we get in and, consequently, we roll out. *The Good News for Modern Man* translates Paul's statement as, "I not only move on, I am leaning forward." Paul is saying that the stance of a Christian is to be leaning forward and moving on. Often we do not lean forward and so we fall out of or fall from Grace. We look at our lives and discover that we really have not made any spiritual progress since the last time we checked. This really is a problem for all of us. Cromwell, the great English general and Christian, had inscribed in the front leaf of his Bible these words: "He who is not getting better is getting worse," meaning that as Christians we must be ever moving on. That is the central unique doctrine that is emphasized in the United Methodist Church. We call it the doctrine of "Christian perfection and sanctification." People sneer, they laugh, and they do not take it too seriously. Methodists were attacked and abused in early days because of this doctrine. But, it is biblical. John Wesley taught that, as followers of Jesus, we must be moving on toward Christian perfection and sanctification. Jesus said in the fifth chapter of St. Matthew, "Be ye therefore perfect as my Father in heaven is perfect." Now perfection does not mean that your life is going to be without error or sin. The word perfection in the New Testament Greek is the word *telios,* which literally means "being full grown," "being mature." It means blossoming. "Be ye therefore maturing to the height of your maturity as your father in heaven is completely matured and perfect."

I remember that my grandmother considered her sanctification to be the only commendation of her whole life. She claimed with great joy that she had been sanctified. By that she meant that she had the Holy Spirit in her life and that he was leading her onward. She meant she was not stalemated nor fossilized nor staying where she was. Every United Methodist minister who has been ordained since the beginning of the Methodist Church has had to stand before an altar and answer the question, "Are you moving on toward perfection?" If after years in the quest, you cannot answer in the affirmative, you may not be ordained in the United Methodist Church. I ask you, "Is your life getting better? Is there beauty and love and joy and excitement? Is there generosity? Is there freedom? Is there faith like you have never had before? Can you at twenty-nine be sure that your life has grown a great deal since you were nine or nineteen? "Are you continuing to grow?" (1 Samuel 2:26)

III. *Continued to Grow in Favor With the Lord and Men*

Eric Erickson, probably the greatest psychoanalyst of our time, has said that the development of primal trust in the first year of a child's life is absolutely necessary if he or she is to become a healthy mature being. Now the Bible is saying that primal trusting of your life to God — to be able to turn loose — is imperative if you are to grow into a mature, healthy Christian. Let me give you an example. Children are not very daring. They are childish. You expect a three-year-old to be childish. For example. they are very conservative. In fact, children are the most conservative human beings in the world. If you ask them. "Do you want me to read you a new story, or read you the old one about the Three Bears?", which one will they request? *The Three Bears.* They want to stay with the same one. "Do you want to sing a new song, or do you want us to sing the same old song?" They will always ask for the same old song. "Would you like to try asparagus or a spinach casserole or would you rather have a Hershey bar?" A Hershey bar. "Do you want to go to a new doctor or do you want to go to the old one?" The old one. "Would you like to go to Paris or would you rather go back to the county fair?" They want to stick to the tried things. They are conservative. They do not want to change a thing.

We expect this of small children and yet we adults go around bragging about our childishness. We say, "I am conservative. I am opposed to anything new." This sounds like a little child. You and I live in such a rapidly changing world that, within the next two years, 23% of all the money you will be spending will be on things that have not yet even been invented. How in the world can you function in a world like that and stay conservative? I hear people say, "I want to keep things just like they are, so tell me the story of *The Three Bears,* do not tell me any new one."

I want things just like they used to be. Nevertheless, we are not consistently like that. I am not that way. When I go to a doctor to have surgery, I do not want him to hit me in the head with a hammer like they did in 5 B.C., nor do I want a surgeon to give me a slug of corn whiskey or say, "Well, grit your teeth and bite on this stick." I want to go to a doctor who uses the newest anesthesia, the newest procedure, the best methods.

I want the newest ways because I have been taught by Christ that I am supposed to live by faith and be daring. Jesus said, "Come and follow me and count not the cost." He said to us, "The old will pass away and behold all things will become new." The Bible teaches us that the riches of Christ are unsearchable. Why then should I think that I have discovered all that there is about Christ and try to keep things just like they are if the riches of Christ are unsearchable?

The mark of maturity shows on one who is willing to be daring.

Jesus said, "Come and follow me knowing not where you are going, count not the cost." Christopher Columbus discovered a new world. Why? Because, he was willing to do something different, something that had never been tried.

Many of us have read James Mitchner's book, *Hawaii*. If you did not, perhaps you saw the movie. You may remember, he spends about one hundred pages telling us how the island was formed and how it was settled by early primitive natives from the South Sea islands of the Pacific. The native tribe that originally settled it was very deeply religious. They believed they were being led by God to go and discover a new area and settle a new world. They set out with their few possessions in little canoes. Charting their way by the stars, they passed the vernal equinox. Suddenly the stars changed and the sky was filled with all new stars, unfamiliar ones. The old marks were gone. The old tradition, the old landmarks had disappeared and now which way would they go? They panicked and turned to their young king and asked, "O King, we must turn back, we have no more tradition, no more guides." You remember what he said to them as he stood up in that little flimsy canoe in the middle of the ocean. He said to them, "No, we will not turn back but we will sail on, because we are in the hands of God."

That is the kind of faith that a mature person has. There are areas and avenues down which you will go and there will be familiar landmarks, but by faith in God you are willing to sail on, to try the new ways and be led by the spirit into new ways of expressing the Christian Gospel — new ways of worshiping, new ways of serving, new ways because the riches of Christ are unending. "Now the boy Samuel continued to grow in stature and in favor with the Lord and with men."

Jeremiah 31:7-14 *Christmas 2*

The Shepherd Guards His Sheep

At Christmas time, the newspapers are filled with articles by psychiatrists addressing the problem of the depression that Christmas causes. Doctors and counselors are interviewed on television shows about depression at Christmas. One such expert offered the following advice:

1. *Try not to expect too much.*
2. *Find someone else who is lonely and depressed with whom you may share Christmas.*
3. *Don't overspend, give cheaper presents and less expensive parties.*
4. *Drink less.*
5. *Anticipate the depression that accompanies Christmas.*

It is rather obvious that people find themselves in these circumstances because they center their lives around the wrong things. They put their trust in that which depresses rather than in that which comforts and encourages. The psychologist seems to assume that Christmas is centered around parties, presents, and a secular non-religious observance. But, lest you think me a prude or a puritan, let me say that I enjoy Santa, Christmas trees and "dreaming of a white Christmas". I sympathize with "Rudolph The Red Nosed Reindeer," disappointed over not being included with the other reindeer. I feel compassion for him, being left alone at the North Pole.

Now I have experienced some theological questions through the years as I have visited elderly lonely persons in nursing homes at Christmas, and I wonder if it is appropriate or cruel for me to say to them, "Merry Christmas?" Every year but one since I became a pastor, I have had to conduct a funeral service at the Christmas season. Would it be honest and at the same time appropriate for me to say at the funeral service to the family and friends, "Merry Christmas" and "Good Tidings"? When I have left Christmas boxes in the homes of the poor whose house was not as nice as my utility shed, I have questioned if it was theologically sound and lovingly appropriate for me to say "Good Tidings and Merry Christmas."

I suppose all of us have wondered whether or not Christmas could bring joy and hope to all, regardless of their predicament. Can I truly say "Good Tidings" to all? If I can say it only to the affluent, I am a fake and Scrooge is right when he says, "Humbug." Actually, from a theological point of view, Christmas offers more *hope* to persons in bad circumstances. The Christmas message, of the coming of a Savior, is one of hope for those who know they are lost, hope for those who need a Redeemer, and for those who need a Shepherd.

To people in bad circumstances, for whom the world offers no hope, Jeremiah says, "Cheer up, I bring you good tidings." Instead of despair and depression, Jeremiah says "sing with joy, shout out with praise and joy for the Lord has saved you."

Jeremiah speaks of the immediate return of the children of Israel from their exile. He speaks with hope and encouragement of their being saved from their lostness in a strange culture. He speaks of their being delivered from those foreign ways and land and reunited with all their people and returned to Zion. He speaks of God, the "saving One," and of the "remnant;" of God ransoming and paying for the release of Jacob and all his descendants, Jeremiah says all this with hope, giving graphic pictures of how it will be, and the feeling of joy and happiness that will reign in their hearts. Now he keeps explaining everything that will happen, using the symbol of God as our Shepherd. He seems to be saying that whether we are depressed or not depends on knowing our Savior as "The Good Shepherd." To these herdsmen the analogy of the Shepherd gathering up the scattered sheep says it all! Shepherds and the "Good Shepherd" are the dominant symbols of the Christmas season. No wonder Handel in his "Messiah" saw this as the dominant idea regarding the Messiah concept.

The Bible refers to "The Good Shepherd" more than eighty times. It is the symbol that the Bible uses above all others. And it is hard for you and me really to understand the significance of that. In fact there is no word in the English language comparable to the word "Shepherd" in the Hebrew: consequently, we never grasp the meaning of that word, because you and I do not understand how essential and how important a shepherd was. Then too, we cannot comprehend it because we presume that the area of Bible times was like North America, but it was not. Some of us who have been to Israel make the mistake of presuming that Israel in Bible days was like it is today. It was not. It was nothing but a land of mountains, rock, stone and desert. Only recently, with American money, has Israel been able to irrigate by piping water from the Mediterranean Sea. Today it is green, but there was not much grass and very little water in those days. The terrain of Israel at times made it impossible for any wild animal that lived off the grass even to survive. For sheep to survive, it was imperative that a shepherd direct them to the grass and to the water.

When I was in college, I went through a cynical period. I used to get resentful about that sheep symbol — the very idea that the Bible would insinuate that human beings were like stupid, witless sheep. I resented even more the very idea the Bible would say that a good, beautiful, strong man like Jesus would give his life for stupid, witless sheep. What a waste! Then I began to realize that my sins of insecurity, selfishness, blindness, and lack of concern for others were the same frailties as the sheep, that I really was like a straying and lost sheep.

A student from the University sat in my office once and said to me, "I am lost, confused, and do not know what I want to do with my life." He characterized his predicament by saying, "I am like a sheep without a shepherd." Let us look at what the Bible means and what Jesus was implying when he said. "I am The Good Shepherd."

I. Provides For Us

One of the most beautiful verses in all the Bible is: "The Lord is my Shepherd, I shall not want." Sheep do not have to beg for what they want or need. The shepherd gives it to them without the sheep having to beg. In fact, he anticipates their every need. God as the Good Shepherd provides for all our needs — heat, food, beauty and peace. All we need do is claim it. A former parishioner who is a soil conservationist told me one day that, as he sat in his truck looking out over a large field of corn ready to be harvested, he saw a fantastic miracle, the miracle of God feeding 10,000 people. He went on to explain that, though this miracle had taken perhaps two months to be completed, it *was* a miracle. For the first time in his life he realized that he could not distinguish an "act of nature" from a "miracle" by the length of time it took to be performed. He reminded me that God could speed up the same process. Instead of the process taking two months, it could take two seconds — and then we would say it was "a miracle." Or, God could take a miracle and lengthen it to two months — and then we would say it was "natural."

Jesus goes on to say that "the Good Shepherd lays down his life for the sheep," not just literally but figuratively. Jesus did not merely give his life for us by dying on the cross. His actual death did not take very long. He gave his life for us *by the way he spent his life.* Whatever you spend you life and time doing is what you "give your life" for. Each of us is dying minute by minute. For example, if you spend a large portion of your life making money, when your funeral service is held they can say that you gave your life for money. If you spend most of your time practicing your backswing or your serve or cultivating the grass in your yard, they will have to say that you died for your golf game, for tennis, or for your lawn. Jesus gave his life for us because every minute of his ministry was spent for others — for us. So, even if he hadn't died on the cross, we could still have said that he died and gave himself *for us.* Yes, "The Good Shepherd" means that God provides for us.

II. Protects, Guides and Controls Us

The shepherd does not run away when the wolf comes like a hireling would do. You and I, we belong to Him, and we have value to Him. A hireling is someone who is just hired to look after the sheep and would run at the first sign of danger because they do not belong to him nor do they have value to him.

When I was in college, I drove a Railway Express truck during the holidays. One of my duties was to drive the truck to the nearby train station some ten miles away and make the weekly delivery of silver to the banks. We did not have an armored truck or guard, just me — a skinny, freckled-faced, bushy-headed boy. Insurance regulations required that I take one bag into the bank at a time. I had to carry a pistol in one hand and a bag in the other. Some of my friends used to kid me about my daring and dangerous job. I would say, "Listen. if someone would come up behind me and stick their little finger in my back, they would not have to ask me twice for that money. In fact, I would ask them where they wanted me to put it." That money did not belong to me nor was it valuable enough for me to give my life for it.

We belong to "The Good Shepherd" and he values you and me. He is not like a hireling. He will not run. He will lay down his life for the sheep. He protects us.

In Eastern lands, shepherds do not herd the sheep as we do here in the Western part of the world. They lead them. They walk out ahead and the sheep follow along behind. On my tour in Israel, I was explaining this to a group of persons at the sheep auction. As our bus left, we passed a man driving his sheep. One of the ladies on our bus, pointing her finger, said, "See, you are wrong because that shepherd is driving his sheep." She thought she had caught me in an error. I explained to her that that man was not a shepherd but the butcher driving them to the slaughter house.

In other words, Jeremiah is saying the Shepherd can lead us through any kind of perilous situation — through dangerous places, even in the valley of the shadow of death. As I write this, I realized that I really had not depended upon that in my own life but rather that I, like many of you, had been attacking only symptoms of our society rather than the cause. I have only been hacking at the outward symptoms of drugs and alcohol and corruption, the educational system, war, racism, and the other problems. I really have stopped short when I have looked to governors or city councils or legislators to control these problems. I needed to have turned the problems over to "The Good Shepherd", who could and can lead us through perilous times and who is the only one who can take care of these problems. We might even change some of these people and some of these institutions momentarily, but neither you nor I have the power to change these persons and these institutions completely and permanently. What we need to do is to bring them all under the Lordship of Jesus Christ, "The Good Shepherd" who can lead them. He can do that to all the complex problems of our day if we would realize the power of The Good Shepherd who can guide us.

Then, we need to remember that sheep were very near-sighted. They could only see for about twenty-five feet at the most. So, they constantly oriented themselves by the sound of their shepherd's voice.

If they could not hear his voice, they became very frustrated and tense. When the shepherd needed to lie down and rest, he would usually sing or occasionally call out to the sheep to keep them from becoming insecure and to keep them from straying. They had no fences in those days. The way the sheep were able to determine their limits was by the sound of their shepherd's voice. If they were getting outside the range of their shepherd's voice, they were going out too far.

You and I live in a world that seems to have lost its moral limits. We also might remember that the limits should still be the same for our morality. When we are outside the Shepherd's voice, then we are too far out. We are beyond the limit. If you do not hear God speaking to you, if you are beyond the sound of His voice, then you are outside His moral limits.

Clarence McCarthy tells of an old shepherd whose wife died in childbirth, leaving him a daughter who was the apple of his eye. He loved her more than anything. Everyday she would go to the fields with him to tend the sheep. She loved better than anything to hear her dad call the sheep. Years passed and she grew up and went off to the big city to go to school and work. Letters came for a while and then no letters at all. Rumors returned that his daughter was in the wrong places with the wrong people. She was working as a common prostitute. He had no address for her, but nevertheless he went to the huge city of over a million people to try and find her. He walked up and down every street inquiring of her whereabouts. Finally, he got the idea that she knew the sound of his voice, so he began walking down every street giving his "sheep call" until one day he went to a street and she was within the range of his voice. She could not resist it and out into the street she ran and into the open arms of her father, the shepherd.

Unite Scattering Sheep

Hirelings will let the wolf come in and scatter the sheep, but the Good Shepherd has sheep "that are not of this fold," and he will gather them also and make one flock. He will unite us. Too long we have lived in a world divided with Bamboo Curtains, China Walls, Iron Curtains, demilitarized zones, and Gaza Strips, divided between sects — Jews and gentiles, black and yellow, red and white. Paul says in Ephesians, "In Christ we are all united." And, he says in the next chapter of Ephesians, "Those that are far off are now brought near. We will become one flock under one shepherd." That is the answer to our international crisis. That is the answer to the problem of ecumenicity.

The day after Martin Luther King was murdered, my congregation and I attended a memorial service at a black Baptist church. I was sitting in a body of ministers on the second pew next to a Roman Catholic priest who was serving at that time under one of the most conservative bishops in all of Roman Catholicism. After the service was underway, the black minister decided that it was a good occasion to celebrate communion. He came down from the pulpit and pointed at me and the priest and said, "I want you two to come and help me administer communion." The Catholic priest nervously looked at me, then said, "Oh, what the heck. This is a first for a lot of things today — black and white and Protestant and Catholic worshiping together."

I have a relative of mine who, from time to time, some people accuse of being on the fanatical side. She is always giving me material to read. I confess that some of it I read and most of it I do not read. I was on a plane on my way back from preaching in Arkansas and I pulled out a sermon she had given me. It was a sermon preached by a pastor at the Evangelical Church in Greenville, South Carolina, an independent church, the sort that believes all churches are wrong except theirs. This is what the pastor wrote:

> *In the present day visitation of the Holy Spirit in the church of Jesus Christ is labeled the "Charismatic Renewal". People who were once divided, both ministry and laity by our different doctrines concerning the gift of the Holy Ghost, are now coming together as one body in the life of the Holy Spirit. "We have been all made to drink into one Spirit." (1 Corinthians 12:13) In the present day outpouring of the Holy Spirit according to the promise given, "And it shall come to pass in the last days, saith God, I will pour out of my Spirit upon all flesh . . . " (Acts 2:17) All of us, regardless of our doctrine on the baptism of the Holy Spirit, are having to eat a little crow. The Lord is not pouring out his Spirit, baptizing believers, according to any one of the prescribed ways of the doctrines of men. He is baptizing Catholics, Episcopalians, Lutherans, Presbyterians, Baptists, Pentecostals, and even Methodists. The Lord is not paying much attention, if any, to doctrines about the baptism of the Holy Ghost that have divided us,*

> *but he is pouring out his Spirit upon all flesh, and his Spirit is bringing us together in one body, with one Lord.*

Wow! You know, I hardly needed the plane to come on home. Fantastic! An independent, sectarian preacher saying that we are all going to be made one flock under one shepherd and that it is not going to come about by organizational structure, not by new ecclesiastical revamping, but by all of us letting Jesus become "the Good Shepherd." "Other sheep I have that are not of this fold, they shall hear my voice and come and be one flock." What a great day that will be!

I went to hear *The Messiah* with one of the most brilliant professors I ever studied under in graduate school at Duke. He was an older gentleman and a man I honored and admired. The choir sang the part where Handel speaks about "The Shepherd" and Jesus being "The Good Shepherd" of the sheep and then moved on into the Hallelujah Chorus. "The front of the professor's shirt was wet with his tears but a smile radiated through and he looked at me and said. "That is my Savior and my Shepherd they are singing about."

Yes, if he is my Shepherd, then he makes me a part of his flock, and he says, "There will only be one flock because I will bring all the other sheep, even those that are not of this fold, unto one fold. They shall hear my voice and come and be one flock."

Jesus truly is "The Good Shepherd"!

Isaiah 60:1-6   Epiphany

The Narrow Way Broadens Us

I grew up with the "anti-Epiphany heresy" that says being a Christian and being narrow are synonymous. Heresies are caused by people who try to make conclusions about the faith even though they know little about the Bible. Knowing little about the Bible, I was controlled by the terrible fear and apprehension that if I became a Christian I would be endangered by narrow-mindedness. It was an enlightenment when I began to read the Bible for myself and discover that the Epiphany lessons taught the opposite.

Now there is the profound thought that has been here long before Christianity arrived that one has to enter a narrow way in order to enter into a broader perspective. For example, Plato in his *Republic* shared with us a simile of the cave man which is symbolic of all persons. The cave man lived in a hole in the ground. He thought that the only world there was was this world in which he lived. He thought the only light there was was the light that came from his flickering little campfire. Someone came through a narrow entrance into the shaft in which he lived and said to him, "Hey, if you will go through this narrow hole to the outside, there is a huge, vast world and universe reaching out endlessly into space, and there is a sun that is so bright, a light so brilliant that it makes your little campfire look dim." Plato says that the cave man, symbolizing us, picked up his club and clubbed the messenger to death for two reasons. First, the cave man refused to leave his cave of darkness and enter the narrow, small tunnel to find a more expansive kind of life. Secondly, he refused to admit there was a light far brighter than the one he currently enjoyed.

A recent television episode about coal miners told about a cave-in and a group of the miners stranded in a certain shaft, boxed in, waiting and hoping to be rescued from the outside. Finally, rescue came from the outside when rescuers dug a narrow tunnel into that large room in which they waited. If they would enter that little tunnel, they could follow it outside, to where their loved ones awaited them, and where the sun shone brightly. And by entering that narrow way, they could save themselves and enlarge their universe. Without hesitation they crawled through the narrow tunnel, knowing that it led to something broader. This is an analogy of the paradox in the Bible. It says to us that we must enter by the narrow way, the narrow tunnel. "Straight is the way and narrow." But after you have entered and found the Christ, the Light, it enlarges your whole life. Attitudes and relationships, instead of becoming more narrow, become more liberal, more tolerant, more understanding, and more expansive.

No one can say of a "born again" person, "He or she is a narrow-minded Christian." No one can say that because you really can't be narrow-minded and be a Christian! Now there might be someone who is in the narrow way, trying to find Christ, but hasn't yet found him. Consequently, they are narrow in everything they do and think because they are in the passage which is narrow. There is no broad way there; it is narrow.

I have known people going through the narrow passage of alcoholism. At first, they thought they were enjoying a broad unrestrained life but it wasn't; it was narrow. They could not do what they wanted to do. There were times they did not want to drink excessively, but they did. They lost control of their lives. It was a narrow way they followed. But once they found Christ they discovered a broad kind of living. This is what the story in Epiphany is talking about. The star or the light mentioned in Isaiah 60 was used as a symbol for the announcement of the coming of the Lord. In that day they believed that the world was flat. So when they talked about a star or light in the heavens, they were talking about a symbol that could be seen from every corner of the earth.

The symbol of the star says that the truth and revelation of God has expanded to all the world, that all might come and see. But the coming is a very narrow way. You can't just pick out any star. There is one single star or light. It is a "special" revelation. And you can't just go any way. You must follow the way it goes. It is straight and it is narrow, and it leads to the small confines of a little town, a small barn, with a small infant in it, all of it taking place in a small country on a small planet in this small universe. This event is trying to say to you that the religion of Jesus' day was expanded by being made small. Do you understand that?

Isaiah 60:1-3:

> *Arise, shine; for your light has come,*
> *and the glory of the Lord has risen upon you.*
> *For behold, darkness shall cover the earth,*
> *and thick darkness the peoples;*
> *But the Lord will arise upon you,*
> *and his glory will be seen upon you.*
> *And nations shall come to your light,*
> *and kings to the brightness of your rising.*

By reducing it, by narrowing the truth of Judaism to the Messiah, it was at the same time expanding it to all the world. For example, when you summarize something, it doesn't mean that you have necessarily narrowed it. You might have taken a very wide concept and reduced it to a few words or a definition.

They asked Jesus if he could reduce or define all the teachings of the Holy Scriptures to a few words. He answered. "Yes, Thou shalt love the Lord thy God with all thy heart, with all thy soul, and with all thy mind and thy neighbor as thyself." He reduced it to that one brief concept but there is nothing narrow about it. I saw a TV program about a tidal wave that was going to hit a beach in seven minutes. It told how one policeman had to clear off the beach in seven minutes. It took thirty minutes to tell the episode that took place in the seven minutes. Have you ever had your wife take twenty minutes to explain something that only took one minute to happen? That doesn't mean that it wasn't an expansive idea or experience. It means that you have reduced it or else she has taken something that was reduced and expanded it. This is what the star or light of Epiphany means. This is what it is all about: by a narrow way you find God who is all in all. It is the opening or birth passage into the most expansive kind of world view you could possibly conceive. It dosn't make you narrow, but it explodes the whole concept of your attitudes, your thoughts. your relationships, your feelings, your forgiveness, your tolerance, your love, and your hope.

Whether or not Isaiah 60:1-6 is a prophecy of the light bringing wise men from the east on camels, bringing gifts of gold and frankincense to the King of Judah, is not germane to this passage. This passage teaches the truth that God reveals himself through the one and only light, and that following the light leads to the broad revelation of God to all people and all nations. The message is, "The Glory of the Lord shall be revealed and all flesh see it." The scholars of the first century claimed that the three wise men were Babylonian astrologers. These gentiles believed the stars determined one's whole life. That was their religion. Astrology says that your life is determined by the relationships of stars to one another and in what relationship they are to each other at certain times. But notice: the Christmas story says there was only *one* star out of all the other stars that you were supposed to follow. And the outcome of your life is not determined by its relationship to other stars but by its relationship to this child, Jesus, who was born in that one spot. He is a singular answer to the vast problems of the whole world — narrow yet expansive.

Marco Polo wrote in his diary about having discovered the village from which the wise men or the three kings supposedly came. He tells how he interviewed the villagers, and how they told about how their grandfathers and great-grandfathers spoke about these three kings who left their village to go to this country down near the Jordan River to find this new King of the Jews. He says that the people in the village still spoke about these three kings; that one of them was young, one was middle-aged, and one was older. And the young one came back and said, "Oh, he is a young king filled with enthusiasm and daring." The middle-aged king came back and said, "Well, he's young enough to have vitality but he's old enough to have maturity." The older king came back and said, "He is a man wise of experience and possesses the wisdom of the ages." Now you can conclude that man makes out of Jesus what he wants to make out of him. But that is not the point. The point is that Christ is for all people of all ages of all races and of all nations. He is for all the world. That is the whole story of Epiphany, that a star or light being set in the sky tells us that the Messiah in the small confines of a manger is for the whole universe. To take place, it requires that the babe to be born, enter through a small passage of the mother, into the expansiveness of this world.

To be born again you must go through the narrow way. But if you have been born again in Christ your whole life has expanded, including your attitudes and hopes. The Bible reveals that everytime someone had an experience with Jesus. it broadened them. Take old narrow-minded Peter, for example. He thought everyone else was wrong but himself. But Peter had a vision that night, praying on the rooftop at the house of the tanner. He really was born again in that moment. The Bible says the next morning he then went over to Caesarea to the home of Cornelius, who was a Roman officer and a gentile and an enemy. No Jew allowed himself to enter a gentile home. He would be unclean. It was to break all the religious laws. But Peter, now that he had been "born again", went over to his enemy's home and told him about Jesus and baptized all the members of the family. Or you remember Paul. He, too, was narrow-minded until he really knew Christ and was born again. He had that experience on the Damascus Road, and he was born again. At Troas he experienced a vision which said, "Come over to Macedonia." He became so broad that he went over to Europe to minister and to evangelize people like us. Once he had been born again, it broadened him.

I. There Was Just One Star

"Arise shine, for *your* light has come." There was just one star, one light that we are supposed to follow. The problem with most of our lives is that they are filled with multiple lights or stars. We follow multiple stars and lights and it causes confusion after confusion. We are always trying to witness to different things. We try to witness to the fact that we are smart, clever, shrewd, charming, dedicated, good, idealistic, realistic, and pragmatic. And we don't even know what we are, who we are. We follow all kinds of stars. The Bible says the only way to experience Jesus is to follow the "One Light", the one way. Paul Tillich reminded us of this in his sobering definition of religion when he said that "religion is man's ultimate concern." It is his prime concern, the one thing, the one star out of all the others he follows. If we don't do that, if we try to be so many things to so many people, we'll end up terribly frustrated.

Remember the man Jesus met, the one living in the tombs? He was insane. He came to Jesus and Jesus asked, "What is your name?" He said, "My name is Legion" which means 'many.' I have no singular light. That is why I am insane."

Jean-Paul Sartre, the French existentialist philosopher and playwright, wrote a play entitled "Kene," which is about a professional Shakespearean actor, who for 37 years played a different role on the stage every night. One night he was Othello, one night Macbeth, one night King Lear, one night Romeo. Finally after thirty-seven years, in a sobering monment in his dressing room, he asked himself the ultimate question. "Who am I? Am I King Lear? Am I Macbeth? Am I Romeo? Who am I?"

Yes, the light is a singular way. Following a singular star, we can find the singular answer. But remember: the narrow way opens into a broad life. That is where we find unity. We don't find unity by putting a bunch of denominations together into one denomination or organizational structure. If every denomination would make one witness to "The One Light" which is Jesus Christ, then we would be unified. When you have narrowed it down to that one "ultimate concern," you have expanded your faith to include all.

Paul had that problem at Mars Hill. He stood before the great philosophers of Athens, and he tried to impress them with the broadness of his philosophy. He talked about the various gods that were represented there. Now Paul was a brilliant man, but he had no singular thought in his sermon. He left there and no one was converted to the Christian faith. Paul promised from that time forward, he would only preach one singular thing — Jesus Christ, the one-time Light.

II. Broadening Unites and Narrowing Expands

Isaiah goes on to say in the fourth verse, "They all gather together, they come to you." We need to realize that the broadening effect is that which *does unify*. In the narrowing of our way and discipline, our lives are expanded. The broadening process unites us into one, and the narrowing is what expands us. We need to realize that the world into which this prophecy came was a narrow world, a world filled with all kinds of divisions and all kinds of walls, a division between Jew and gentile. Even the temple had four different walls to separate four different groups of people: the gentiles were on one side, the Jews on another, the priest on one side, the people on another. Judaism was a narrow way, a narrow religion. There was no acceptance of other religions, cultures, people. There was war and strife. But Isaiah says that the light comes to bring all together.

Later Ephesians says that "in Christ those that are far off are brought near." Wise men from afar were brought near to this one spot. In Christ all are made one. You say, "Oh, yes, it says that but it hasn't happened. In our world there are all kinds of divisions, all kinds of war, Iron Curtains, and Bamboo Curtains, Southern and Northern Korea, Northern and Southern Ireland, East and West of the River Jordan, black and white, liberal and conservative, Protestant and Catholic, Jew and Arab."

There are divisions in our day and yet we live in a day in which the world grows smaller daily. I can travel around the world today in less time than my grandfather could go to the county seat. Astronauts now go around the world in a matter of minutes. It used to take my grandfather half a day to go to town. Can you conceive how much smaller the world is? I can hear it squeak everyday as it shrinks.

I can remember when I was a boy in a little church of 100 members; it would take maybe a week to get the announcements to every member. Now in less than five minutes, we can send a message to every human on the earth. Barefoot shepherd boys in Algiers, running up the path chasing their sheep, hear within seconds on the transistor radios in their pockets what happens in the United States only seconds after it happens. We live in a small world. You can leave Chicago, for example, on Sunday morning at 12:15 a.m. and fly in less than forty-five minutes to Detroit, arriving on Saturday night. When you get there, the time will be fifteen minutes earlier than when you left. Your friends that meet you at the airport ask you what time you left and you could say, "Well, I left tomorrow." That's how small the world is.

There is a necessity that this world that has shrunk must be broadened to the point where it includes us all, so that we might become one. Christ said, "If I, the Light of the World be lifted up, I will draw all men unto myself." That is a promise. and it works. I can hardly conceive how you and I can exclude other people, because if you have really been born again in Christ, life can't be narrow; it will be inclusive.

What is the obligation of the faith? It begins with the narrowness of a singular star or light to be followed in a singular way to a singular spot, to a singular Messiah who is the singular answer to all the world's problems. And it broadens and explodes our whole life until we reach out even unto all the world.

I was in Chicago and wanted to go to the Chapel in the Sky, which is a sort of Methodist shrine. It was the tallest building in Chicago. It is on top of the Chicago Temple, which is a Methodist Church. I had heard so much about it, but when I got up there, I was disillusioned. It was a small chapel. I sat there, trying to ponder why it was considered a significant place. Then I noticed that the stained glass windows had little cranks on them, like Miami windows which can be cranked open. The main window had a hand in it. I wondered about the meaning of that symbol. I walked to the window and cranked it out. Out of the confines of that little chapel, through that small narrow window, I could see the whole city of Chicago lying before me: 3,000,000 people coming through the confines of a small window!

Then I realized what that stained glass window was supposed to say to me. The hand represented the hand of God. As the ballad says, "He's got the whole wide world in His hands." One hand only, but how broad it is. That is what the star of light does. It leads us in a narrow way through the birth chamber of a small tunnel that opens into an expansive new kind of a life. That is what being born again means, and what Epiphany is about.

Arise, shine, for your light has come. Lift up your eyes round about and see.

Isaiah 61:1-4   Epiphany 1 — Baptism of Our Lord

The Effect of Christ's Coming

After every Christmas some disappointed or cynical person will say, "Christmas came and went; nothing changed. No one really changed." It always makes me think of this rough, old guy who, one night at a revival meeting, went up and gave a testimony about his life. He said, "Brothers and sisters, you all know that I have not been what I ought to have been, and that I've stolen hogs, gotten drunk, and told lies. I've been playing poker and gambling and I've been cussing and swearing. But one thing I can stand here and testify to is that, through all of this, one thing I haven't done; I ain't never lost my religion." I am sure of that! I am also sure that the religion he followed and practiced was not Christianity. What kind of effect does Christmas make on our lives?

In Isaiah 61:1-4 we have the story of people asking the prophet the same question. They said, "You know, we have been hoping, waiting, and longing for the Messiah to come. We would like to ask one searching question. What kind of characteristics will this Messiah have? To whom will He come? The second question is: What makes this an Epiphany lesson? Isaiah answered, "Yes, that is a valid question. Why would you long for someone to come unless you knew that he could change your life and change the world?" So he begins in this 61st Chapter to tell them what the Messiah will be like. Most of us, when we study the book of Isaiah, pick up certain terminology. The term most of us usually pick up is "suffering servant." Isaiah portrays Christ and the Messiah as the "suffering servant." That is a good description. It is the same kind of description that Henry Nouwen, the famous Jesuit theologian, is trying to describe in his book, *The Wounded Healer*. Yes, God did suffer. The Messiah was a suffering human being, but one who in his suffering was concerned more about other peoples' suffering. He was a "wounded healer." Now some children of Israel were in captivity for almost two hundred years. They were slaves partially set free. A few had come back to Jerusalem. They thought getting to Jerusalem would be the answer to all their problems. But they discovered that Jerusalem was desolate; there was mismanagement in the local government. There was no holy Temple. They were disillusioned and disappointed. They were hurting.

Isaiah says it is to that kind of person in that kind of a situation, to whom the Messiah comes. He is a "wounded healer." He is a "suffering servant," one who serves those who suffer. So Isaiah tells them these are the characteristics the Promised One will have. Jesus accepted all these portraits of the Messiah. In fact, He was asked, "What and who are you? What kind of a Messiah are you going to be?" In the fourth chapter of Luke's Gospel, He answered by quoting these same four verses. "The Spirit of the Lord will be upon him and he will preach good news to the poor. He will heal the brokenhearted and those that are captive. He will set free and declare this is the acceptable year of the Lord." Later on, John the Baptizer sent his disciples to Jesus to ask, "Are you the One? Are you the Promised One or should we look for another?" Again Jesus quoted those same verses. "Go and tell John the poor hear the Gospel preached; the blind see; those with broken hearts are healed; those that are captured are set free." We know that Jesus understood himself as fulfilling these characteristics. First of all, he will be anointed by the Spirit of God so that he will preach good news to the poor and to the underprivileged. He will heal the broken-hearted. He will set free those who are prisoners and open the jails and prison cells of all those who have been captured. Last of all, he will announce and proclaim that this is the acceptable year of the Lord.

I. Bring Good News to the Poor and Afflicted

Isaiah says He will bring good news to the poor. Actually the coming of Christ, the Advent or what you and I call Christmas, is only for the poor! There is no message in Advent for the rich, only the poor and the afflicted. Who needs a Savior except someone who is lost? Who needs a healer unless they are wounded? Who needs one to bring to them what they need unless they are poor? Who but the poor would ever search and long for the answer to all their problems? Jesus said the same thing in the Beatitudes: "Blessed are the poor in Spirit for only they shall see the Kingdom of God." That always hurts me when I read it because I know I am rich. I have all I need to eat, more than one suit of clothing. I am rich and yet I am reminded that the story of Christmas has no meaning to the rich, only to the poor. It is good news to the poor only! The recognition of his coming was revealed to the poor, humble shepherds. It was a woman named Anna, who worked as a maid around the Temple, to whom the Christ-Child was revealed. It was to a Temple beggar, Simeon, who considered himself a prophet as he sat outside the Temple gate and begged for alms, that there came the revelation of who that Child was. He was revealed to kings from the east who were poor in spirit, suffering from depravity or spirituality.

Christianity is a faith for the underdog, the underprivileged, the needy. How does the Liberator come? How can he help us if we are so poor? He is King of Kings and Lord of Lords, whose riches are unsearchable. The Talmud, writings which for Jews are the most sacred scriptures outside the Old Testament, talk about the coming Messiah, the longing for him. There is a legend in the Talmud to this effect:

> *Rabbi Joshua ben Levi came upon Elijah, the prophet, while he was standing at the entrance of Rabbi Joshua ben Levi's cave. He asked Elijah, "When will the Messiah come?" Elijah replied, "Go and ask him yourself." "Where is he?" "Sitting at the gates of the city," said Elijah. "How shall I know him?" "He is sitting among the poor, covered with wounds. The others unbind all their wounds at the same time and then bind them up again. But he unbinds them one at a time and binds it up again, saying to himself, 'Perhaps I shall be needed; if so, I must always be ready so as not to delay for a moment.' "*

He is the suffering servant, the wounded healer, always wanting to heal. You know, the poor people today believe there is no way a rich man can go to heaven. That is not even a debatable question among poor people. Ask any deprived person on the street anywhere, "Will a rich person go to heaven?" They will tell you, "No!"

I remember the first time I preached in a prison. After the sermon I invited questions from the prisoners. Can you guess which question all the prisoners asked me? It was theologically rather profound, I thought. They wanted to know, "Can a prison guard ever go to heaven?" And I had to say, "No." Can a rich man go to heaven? No! Jesus said, "It will he harder for a rich man to enter heaven than for a camel to go through a needle's eye." I explained to the prisoners that only by the grace of God will anyone get to heaven. Only the poor, only those who may have worldly riches but realize their depravity, who live perhaps in a $125,000 residential section but know that they live in a ghetto of spirituality — only the poor who know they are poor — can be saved.

You have heard the story of the Methodist minister who died and went to heaven, and for his reward St. Peter gave him a little Chevette, a four-on-the-floor, stick shift. He enjoyed it for a while, "spinning off" at every intersection, until he saw a man down the street who, he thought, had not lived a very good life, but was driving a Buick. The Methodist minister was irate! He went to St. Peter and complained. The next day he saw a fellow he thought was even worse, riding around in a Cadillac. He really was upset about that. Every day he went back complaining. "It's not fair. I deserve better!" Finally, one day he stopped bothering St. Peter. A week passed and he had not come to complain, so St. Peter wondered what had made him satisfied with the Chevette. So he want to see him and asked, "Why are you now satisfied with your Chevette?" The preacher answered, "Well, I admit I was pretty upset, until the other day I saw my Bishop on a skateboard." It is only to the poor that He comes, only to the poor, and we need to understand that. "The last shall be first and the first last."

I was reading an article recently in "Good News Magazine." It is a renewal group in the Methodist Church for evangelical, fundamental, scriptural holiness. It was written by the executive secretary of "Good News." It is not from a social gospelist, my friend; it is from a fundamental evangelical who says that the church's only salvation is to get out there and care for the needy. The title of the article was, "Farewell to Welfare." He talks about the impact of the government's doing away with $18,000,000,000 worth of welfare and the effect it will have on the community. Who will feed them? Who will clothe them? He said the church must! It has one last chance to save itself. He makes the point that the government, from about 1920 to 1970, had to get in the welfare business because the church wouldn't do it. The church was more concerned with surviving as an institution and propagating the institution. But he pointed out that we have another chance, a second chance to feed all those out there now who are hurting and hungry. He said we have that chance for several reasons, and he is glad of it. First, the church can do it for less money and more effectively. Secondly, the social welfare system is impersonal and it takes human dignity away from people. And thirdly, it gives us a chance to witness to the Lord. So we must do it! Jesus said, "I have been anointed to preach the Good News to the poor."

One day when I got out of my Bible Study at 11:00, the secretary said there was no way I could see all the relief applicants which I interview every Tuesday and Thursday from 11:00 a.m. until noon. There were twenty-seven waiting. Most of them had light bills they couldn't pay, no food in their house. It doesn't take long every day from 11:00 — 12:00 to give away several hundred dollars. It is a joy to be able to say to everyone who comes in the office, "Good news, my friends, good news! Jesus came into our lives. Because he preached good news to the poor, we must also, and that is why we are helping you." Money pours in without any solicitation, because people want to follow him who preached good news to the poor.

II. Bind Up the Brokenhearted

Second Isaiah says that he comes to bind up the broken-hearted. Broken hearts exist everywhere — among rich, poor, educated and uneducated. You can't imagine the kind of grief that is going on in some people's lives. They grieve over a lost job, the inability to make enough money to feed their family, over a loved one who had died, over a child whose life has gone astray. Grief, all kinds of grief, over our failure to live up to what we know we could be and should be. In her famous book, *Death and Dying,* Kubler Ross says that perhaps the most important thing you could do for someone who grieves is just *be there* and comfort them by being a part of their lives.

Dr. Bob Nenno, a psychiatrist and a very good friend of mine, was speaking one day to our ministerial association about a matter he and I had discussed several times in private. He was speaking of how at Christmastime, as a result of a secular world's concept of Christmas, people are inflicted with all kinds of emotional problems that they don't have at other times during the year. Those are multiplied at Christmas. During the Christmas season about 90% of the people go around with their hearts filled with hatred, bitterness and hostility. Why? Because they didn't get everything they wanted. You give the wife a new Buick for Christmas and she wanted a Cadillac. You give her a washing machine and she really wanted a mink coat. Or did you ever see a child who, after he has opened all presents under the tree, has a facial expression that says, "Is that all?" It is the sort of mentality of our day. Or people suffer from all kinds of depression during the Christmas season because of the Christmas message of the secular world. In the beer and wine advertisements, crowds of folks come to your home. If that crowd came to your house, and you had that many people to feed, you would be miserable! But it makes you think that Christmas means being together with family or a crowd of people with a lot of noise. If you get in the crowd, you aren't satisfied. Or if you are a single person or a lonely person who doesn't have any family coming in at Christmastime, you make yourself depressed by thinking that you are supposed to be depressed because you didn't have any company at Christmastime.

Now, the problem is that the church has not proclaimed the Gospel about the coming of Christ. The secular world has introduced everybody to *their* concept of Christmas. We have never told them about the One who comes to bring peace. "Peace, not as the world giveth, give I unto you. Let not your hearts be troubled." Not a crowd of people around you but the comfort of God who says, "Emmanuel, I am with you. You're not alone." Yes, the secular world's concept of Christmas is making people insane. We need to get the message of the Bible to them — the message of what the Promised One would be.

I was wondering how I could explain this to you as I was typing this message. The phone rang. A layman said that, if possible, he would like me to come out to the hospital and see a very prominent physician in our community. By all standards he would be considered the pinnacle of success, a wonderful person (although without any kind of church relationship). He couldn't talk with his professional peers. The only thing they knew to do was to treat his symptoms which were the physical problems of his wife who was dying in the hospital.

Everybody was treating the *symptoms,* not what was really wrong. He was suffering from a broken heart. I had good news to bring to him about the Promised One who comes to heal the brokenhearted. You can have everything in the world and still have a broken heart. Many of us overlook those things.

I heard of a little girl who had a doll that she had had since infancy. It was her favorite doll. But the doll's head got broken, crushed. So she went to the healing service at her church on Sunday night. When the minister gave an invitation for persons to come down to the altar and declare their request for healing, she walked up to the minister and, with tears streaming down her fat cheeks, held up her soiled doll with the broken head. He looked at her and said, "I'm sorry, darling, but we don't heal broken dolls." She said, "What I want to know is do you heal a broken heart?" You see, most of us when we hear the story, like the minister, think that the problem was a broken doll. We aren't sensitive enough to realize that what is hurting people is not the broken dolls, but the broken hearts. He comes to heal the broken heart.

III. Proclaim Liberty to the Captives

Isaiah says he comes to proclaim liberty to the captives, to release from prison those who are in prison. People are imprisoned by all kinds of things — inferiority complexes, prejudices, ignorance, enslavement by alcohol, drugs, sex. A week never passes that I am not talking with someone out in the psychiatric ward, and I say to them, "Hey, you need to try to stop putting on this big front about living in a certain kind of house and getting in such a financial bind. Why do you have to project such an image?" "Oh, I know that," they will say. (I have heard it a hundred times.) "The doctor has told me to turn it loose. But how?" Materialism is like an octopus that has gripped us all. How do we turn it loose? It is not that easy.

I used to go to Alcoholics Anonymous when I was a boy. My dad was a member of AA. We went three or four nights a week. I remember the twelve steps, the first of which is, "Admit we are powerless over alcohol, that our lives have become unmanageable." Everybody has to admit that. "Come to believe that a power greater than ourselves has come to restore us to sanity." Then finally comes the twelfth step: "Having had a spiritual awakening as a result of these steps, we try to carry this message to alcoholics and other persons and practice these principles in all our affairs." In Dicken's *Christmas Carol,* the character Scrooge was imprisoned, locked behind bars, with his wealth, until that night the rescuer came to him and the doors were opened, and he was set free.

IV. Proclaim This the Acceptable Year of the Lord

The Promised One is not "way out there" in the future, not "yet to come," not tomorrow. No, he is now! *Now* is the acceptable year of the Lord.

I began by telling you the ancient legend from the Talmud, about Rabbi Joshua ben Levi. There is an end to that story. The rabbi went to Elijah and asked him, "When will the Messiah come?" Elijah explained to him that he could find the Messiah sitting at the gate with the poor. Rabbi ben Levi went to the Messiah and said to Him, "Peace be unto you, my Master and my Teacher." The Messiah answered, "Peace to you, son of Levi." Finally he asked, "When is the Messiah coming?" "Today," He answered. Rabbi Joshua ben Levi returned to Elijah who asked, "What did he tell you?" "He indeed has deceived me, for he said, 'Today I am coming' and he has not come." To which Elijah said, "This is what he told you, 'Today if you would listen to his voice.' "

That is the Epiphany lesson from Isaiah: today, right now is the acceptable year of the Lord. He who will preach good news to the poor and the afflicted. He who will heal the broken-hearted. He who will set you free from whatever it is that captivates and imprisons your life. He will come right now — *this minute* — if you will only receive him. For this is the acceptable year of the Lord.

Isaiah 62:1-5

Epiphany 2 (Common, Lutheran)
Ordinary Time 2 (Roman Catholic)

Burned Out

A man said to me recently, "I'm just plain 'burned-out' after Christmas. I have lugged the Christmas tree out to the curb, but all the ornaments are still packed in boxes in the spare bedroom. Then there is the end of the year and all that goes along with that . . . the working to stay ahead of inflation and trying to keep from going down during the recession . . . working hard to get through college or get a promotion or get ahead in life." This man was caught in a grinding toil and going through the motions. No wonder we hear a whole lot about "burned-out." Psychologists say it is the result of a conflict of expectations, usually at a subconscious level. We have experienced conflict that we are not what we expected to be, or our life has not accomplished what we thought it should have accomplished. And now we are burned-out. I haven't picked up a women's or a men's magazine or any kind of religious periodical in the last two years that hasn't had an article on the "burned-out" syndrome. Executives in highrise buildings experience it. So do nurses, housewives, teachers, secretaries, farmers, social workers, judges, doctors, and clergymen. In fact, everybody seems to feel some sort of "burn out", which doesn't mean the wick has burned up but the light has gone out.

Many of us remember that maintenance man from Brooklyn who won the world's biggest lottery jackpot: $5,000,000. He did it by picking six lucky numbers. The day after he picked up the money he returned to work. Several days later he wrote, "I said to myself, what kind of nut am I? I'm putting in lightbulbs when I have $5,000,000." Well, that is the same kind of nut all of us are. No matter how much you have, you still have the perennial problem of keeping the lightbulbs in, the light going, and the candle lit. You still have the problem of staying lit up, and we seem to never to get to a point where that is not a problem. That is what we call the "burned-out" syndrome.

Isaiah, when he writes "until her vindication goes forth as brightness, and her salvation as a burning torch," is reaffirming todays Epiphany Scripture. He is saying that the Messiah will be a special light or torch that no darkness or desolation can extinguish. By "burning torch," Isaiah is saying this is a special revelation. There have been all kinds of general revelations about God prior to this. Now there is general revelation and there is special revelation. General revelation can be seen, for example, in the creation. You can look around you, at the world God has made, and see evidence of God. That is general revelation. Reasoning and logic participate in general revelation — they can persuade us of the existence of God and our need for God.

But there is something beyond that. There is the "true light," the "special" revelation which is Christ. And Isaiah is trying to make it clear that this is unique. It is the torch that shall never go out. Even the Word of God, the lamp unto our feet, a light unto our path, sometimes grows dim because of our lack of faith in it. But the true light that lights all the world shall never be extinguished. You must understand how easy it is for general revelations, or for the lesser lights in our lives (upon which quite often our religion is based) to grow dim and go out.

Samuel Miller, the former dean of Harvard Divinity School, writes:

Believing requires a great deal more than mere intellectual assent. A kind of dynamic actuality, a reservoir of positive energy, a strength to pierce beyond the very limits of credibility, is demanded. Faith may fall on evil days, exhaust itself, and what once sustained us then becomes a burden we are forced to carry. Our believing fluctuates as mysteriously as a candle flame in a gusty world.

In Isaiah 62:4 Isaiah speaks of the feelings of being forsaken and desolate. For us forsakenness and desolation could stand for a state of mind, delusion and "burned-outness." Darkness stands for despair, depression, middle-age crisis, adolescence, menopause, professional crisis, spiritual darkness. That is a human reality. These are obvious facts in our lives. The Bible says that the light came into the world but the world knew Him not. But the true light which lightens up all men has come and the world could put it out.

Let's discuss this syndrome that we call burned-outness or desolation. You have read a lot about it. Many of you have suffered a great deal from it. Let us try to diagnose the symptoms of this malady that seems to inflict us in the twentieth century. Let us also try and state what is the disease proper, not just diagnose the symptoms. But most of all, let us then talk about what is the cure. My greatest criticism of most of the sermons I hear is that they spend a great deal of time diagnosing what is wrong with the world and the evils of the world. But I hear very little said about the cure. Let's talk about the cure; *but first,* let's diagnose the problem.

I. Diagnosis of Symptoms

The syndrome which we call the "burned-out" state was first formulated by the novelist Graham Greene in his book, *The Burnt Out Affair.* Since Greene's book, psychologists, theologians and other religious people have adopted that as one of the real syndromes or neurotic tendencies from which all of us seem to suffer. Psychologists tell us that 80% of us suffer from the "burnt-out" syndrome at some time or another in our life. Some people call it the "after-Christmas blahs." One called it "Nada." Ernest Hemingway called it the "black ass." Some call it "middle-age crisis." Some call it despondence and despair. The symptoms are migraines, nervousness, backaches, drinking too much, depression, insomnia, tension, divorce or separation, dropping out of school or whatever. Or we could go on and on. You might not have all these symptoms; you might have only one.

Often it really is described as a feeling of not caring, of numbness, of passive non-resistance, of passive indifference, of saying, "Well, I have done my bit. I have done my share. I am going to retire now and let someone else do it." That is "burned-outness"! Often it reflects itself in religion. People will say to me, "Well, Pastor, I don't know what it is, but I don't have that feeling in my heart that I used to have. The light has gone out. It affects every part of our life. Often the symptoms are that you and I blame outside things or circumstances or persons for our condition. We blame it on our spouses, on the circumstances, on the times, on our job. on our boss. It is easy to say, "If I had more time to myself; if I had a little more time to play golf or to go sailing or fishing, it wouldn't be that way." Or, "If I had another job, another wife, or another husband, it wouldn't be that way." Or, "If the children just didn't make so much noise and didn't get in so many things all the time." Or, "If I could just live somewhere else or in another time."

While many of these "if onlys" might make a difference, the root cause of the problem is the fact that the light has burned out in your life. We need a light that is eternal, that never goes out. That's been the longing of mankind since the beginning of time. The Greeks, with all their various religious legends, saw that as their greatest longing of humanity. That is why and how they formulated the old legend about Mt. Olympus. Once every four years at the Olympics, we get a runner to take the torch supposedly from the eternal flame and carry it to symbolize to the whole world that "there is an eternal torch." Even though they may have lit that torch with a cigarette lighter, a Bic, there is still that hope and that longing that such an eternal light does exist that will never go out.

Tolstoy, in his book, *War and Peace,* lets the character Pierre become Tolstoy. When I read Tolstoy's biography I understood that Pierre was autobiographical. He was a rich man who inherited a lot of farms. He had tried everything from hang-gliding to scuba diving. He tried making more money, running the farms, living a wild, sinful life off at college. You name it, and he had done it. But he reached the point of just being burned-out with no goals left, no joy, no feeling. These are the symptoms. But what is the disease?

II. Disease Proper

Graham Greene in his book, *The Burnt-Out Affair,* describes the main character whose name is Monsieur Queery, an architect of international fame who has built a career to fantastic heights — only to find that now he is the greatest man in his field in the world, but that it is all tasteless and flat. Have you ever reached that point? Strive to reach what you thought was your ambition and your goal, only to find that it tastes like ashes and vinegar. Queery turned his back then on everything — fame, family, honor, wealth — to seek anonymity in the jungle. Finally, he ends up in the heart of the jungle of Africa at a Dominican monastery hospital, given to caring for lepers. I don't know how many of you have ever been around leprosy. It burns wild for awhile and then "burns itself up," leaving you numb with the nervous system gone, no feeling, no smell, nor ability to hear. For the most part these lepers moved about on stumps of feet and carried on as best they could with hands without fingers or with arms without hands. They were all right now. It wasn't contagious any longer. They had been mutilated by it, but there was no pain. There is no pain to leprosy after it has gone through you. They are simply called "burned-out" cases at the hospital. That is where the term comes from. And Queery, this famous architect, soon recognized that he, too, was just a "burned-out" case, burned out by the ravages of civilization, its furious passions and besetting fires of ambition. No emotions are left, no ecstasies desired. He is just numb.

Burned-out means the light has gone out inside of you. Now you never get burned out from working too hard. It is not caused by that. It comes from the stress of the conflicts in your life. It is the lack of meaning in what you are doing. It is the lack of a goal and objective. It is the lack of returning to the fires of your youth to keep the fires kindled and glowing.

Most of all, it's the result of not having burning within you the flame of God, the eternal torch that never goes out. The United Methodist Church picked as its symbol the flame. Why the flame? It is to remind us of that one true light that is eternal and that burns and can never go out. And if you suffer from a burned-out kind of syndrome in your life, it is because you don't have the eternal flame burning within you. The disease is characterized by persons who are ever trying to light up their lives. They are always trying to get "lit up" or "turned on." Maybe it is hang-gliding. That sort of turns me on. Or maybe it is scuba diving. Or marijuana. Or going to the beach or playing golf or watching TV or boozing it up. You search for things to turn you on. The symptoms of our disease are being burned out and looking for some way to be "lit up."

I see it a lot in my profession. Take a man like Albert Schweitzer. He was a good example of a burned-out case. He suffered from it. He was ahead of his time. He was the world's greatest organist, the world's greatest authority on Bach, a Ph.D. in music. He graduated from the Divinity School with a Bachelor of Divinity degree. Then he got a Ph.D. in theology, then an M.D. degree, then a Master of Medicine. He became the greatest authority on tropical diseases in the world. He reached it all by age forty and it was flat, tasteless. So, because of his reverence for life and his protest against the massive ambitions of war and power, he built with his own hands an outpost in an African jungle for the nurturing of the True Light, so that he wouldn't end up burned out like all the rest of the world.

But you can look at other people like Ernest Hemingway or Marilyn Monroe, or nine of the ten richest men in the world who committed suicide because they were burned out. Some people drop out or sail away into the sunset or numb the darkness of their lives with alcohol and drugs.

Gail Sheehy wrote the best seller, *Passages*. I just got her new book. Like everybody else, if it had her name on it I had to read it. It said the same thing the first one said. It is entitled, *The Pathfinder*. But one thing I sensed that she was groping with and couldn't explain was the problem of people getting into the passageway, but having nothing to light up the passageway so they could decide which door to go through and which passage to take. If you are in darkness, even though you knew you needed to go through the passage, it doesn't do you any good unless you have a torch to light up the way you need to go. This is why Jesus said, "I am the light of the world." It is why the Bible says. "He is a light unto our path, a lamp unto our feet." Much of our "burned-outness" is a result of our feeling that we are forced to do something that is imposed on us, like being a doctor because your mother and daddy wanted you to be a doctor. Or having four children because your husband wanted four children. Or having to move to another town because the company said you had to move. That is a sign of our adolescence. It is saying you haven't taken charge of your life. There's nothing wrong with being a doctor because your mother and dad wanted you to be a doctor as long as you choose to be a doctor. There is nothing wrong with being the mother of four children because your husband wanted to have four children, if you have chosen these four children as yours, and you love them. There is nothing wrong with having to move to another town because the company says you have to move, if you choose to be there. The right to choose doesn't mean you get to do what you want to do. The right to choose means that, for the first time in your life, you take charge of your life and you choose what you are doing. That's the way you avoid some of that stress of having to do what you don't want to do.

If there's anybody I get impatient with it is the spoiled, never-grown-up kid who always says, "I don't go to church anymore because, when I was growing up, my parents always made me go." That might be true, but I think, "Why can't you reach adulthood and why can't you take charge of your life and choose to do what your parents taught you to do? It could be your choice." Burned-out is caused by our not taking charge of ourselves. We need to choose what we are doing so that the stress that comes from it is the result of the goals we choose in our lives. Then we won't feel burned out.

III. Cure

Now what is the cure? We have alluded to the burned-outness. It is because we don't have the true light that never goes out in our lives. It is because we haven't taken charge of our lives and chosen what we are doing. We have rebelled because we haven't had the responsibility to take charge of our lives and choose it.

Pierre in *War and Peace* is really Tolstoy. Tolstoy tells about how he had been burned out, how he had everything but really had nothing. He was on this train going nowhere, thinking he would end his life. And he met a man who was a Mason. This man said to him, "Would you like to be brought from darkness to light?" Tolstoy said, "Yes." The man said, "Meet me at the lodge meeting tonight at 9:00?" And he gave him the address. The man said, "And I will bring you from darkness to light, bring you to the great light even in the midst of the lesser lights that fade away." That night Tolstoy went to the meeting and those Masons brought him from darkness into light and he saw for the first time in his life the one great light that stands even among the lesser lights, that never will be extinguished. Tolstoy, from that moment on, became one of the great Christians of all time. The light burned in his life from then on. He had goals, meaning, a future. He knew what he wanted to do with his life. And he left a mark on the world. Light that penetrates beyond the surface, the situation, the circumstances, to the hidden darkness of the inner soul.

When that light comes it shows us what our life is really like, doesn't it? It shows up the things in your life. I'm reminded of a little boy who said, "Mommy, when you die are you going to heaven?" She said, "Yes, and you'll go to heaven, too." Then he started crying and she said, "What is the matter?" He said, "I'm crying because daddy won't go to heaven." She said, "Why do you think daddy won't go to heaven?" He said, "Because he can't leave the store." Think about that.

When the light comes, it shines up the basic realities of what really are our priorities. "He won't go to heaven because he can't leave the store." The torch reveals, not only what we are, but shines on where we are going to go. And that is imperative. If you're going somewhere you need to see where you are going. I remember many a night flying home in a private plane I had chartered to go somewhere to speak. The darkness of the night and the yearning to get back home makes you feel lonely and lost. Then we got near the airport, and we saw the familiar lights of our town. As we approached the airport, all of a sudden, they threw the switches and the lights on the runway flooded our path. When an airplane I'm on is landing, I always pray, "Dear God, don't let that light go out until I have landed." It is a horrible feeling to be flying around in the dark with nothing to light your way.

Do you suffer from a burned-outness, a sort of numbness in your life? Do you seem to have lost all goals and fun in life? Has even the zeal for your profession and your ambition gone out? It doesn't have to be that way. You can have the "burning torch" that enlightens the world.

I remember when I was a boy we used to sing that little song:

This little Gospel light of mine,
I'm going to let it shine.
Don't let Satan blow it out;
I'm going to let it shine.

The one true light that I'm talking about, that lights all the world, including the darkness in our lives, cannot be extinguished because it burns eternally in Christ Jesus. If you don't have that light in your life and that flame burning and flowing, if you are often feeling "burned out", I pray that you will open your heart and your mind and be illuminated by that eternal light.

Nehemiah 8:1-4a, 5-6, 8-10   Epiphany 3 (Common, Lutheran)
                                    Ordinary Time 3 (Roman Catholic)

The Happy Find

For four nights half of America suffered through four and one-half hours of commercials just to view Irvin Wallace's "The Word." It was a movie made from a novel for television. Since the discovery of the Dead Sea Scrolls some twenty years ago, there have been numerous plots of novels written about the possibilities of man discovering new books of the Bible which could either revolutionize the Judeo-Christian faith as you and I know it, or could refute part of what you and I already believe. Since the discovery of the Dead Sea Scrolls, which verified our holy writings, the world has lived with great anticipation of the possibilities of what some new discovery could reveal. Others have lived with the fear that we might find something that would refute our faith.

This past summer, while on vacation I read a novel entitled *The Gemini Expedition,* which was about the discovery in Romania of a scroll that could change, perhaps, the whole world and Christianity. Influential powers fought over possessing the scroll in order either to enrich or destroy the faith. I can remember reading, while in Divinity School, a religious novel written by Arthur Train entitled *The Lost Gospel.* It was about two distinguished archaeologists, one German and one American, who recovered ancient scrolls which turned out to be "the lost gospel," a fifth one for which scholars had searched for 2,000 years.

The plot of "The Word" is interesting and fascinating; it is not unique. In fact, all such interpretations are based on Nehemiah's story of Ezra rediscovering the sacred book of Law. But if you read the novel, *The Word,* or saw the television movie, you would remember that the message that it supposedly unfolds and uncovers was the same message that Matthew, Mark, Luke and John have already unfolded and announced to the world. Wallace's novel assumes a new message, a new discovery that Jesus was the Son of God, was crucified, and rose again and now lives and is present in the world and does great wonders for those who find him. Did this material unveil a new gospel? If you thought it was new, you have not yet heard the real gospel which has the same message. Now, the gospel that Jesus is alive now and among us and can work great wonders in the world is not a new gospel, and yet, it is a lost gospel. Most of the world and most of us really have not responded to this as a fact; consequently, it is as if that gospel had not yet been discovered for us and remains waiting to be excavated, to be found, to be uncovered. You and I have lost and buried the holy book.

The word "gospel" means good news, a great press release, good news to the whole world. Yet, you and I have buried it and lost it under the sands of indifference. We have hidden it in the cryptic tombs of our own lack of response and the fact that we have not yet met this resurrected, alive Lord, about whom it speaks. The gospel is lost to most people in the modern world because they are indifferent to it and therefore ignorant of it. So it sounds like a new gospel, a new find. You have noticed how new, born again Christians act as if they have found something new in the Bible. They have! But most of us have left the gospel hidden in some ancient, cryptic catacomb or tomb, buried under the sands of our own indifference.

It was the first day of the seventh month . . . it was New Year's Day 397 B.C. and one of Israel's Holy Days and sacred gatherings of the people for worship. Apparently, for a long time and for whatever reasons, the "Book of the Law", the sacred Scriptures, had been lost from the people. Maybe Ezra was the curator of the scroll, maybe it had only recently been found in a jar under the old ruins. However, none of these conjectures are important to the event. The significance was a back-to-the-Word-of-God reform, or as we would describe it, a reformation consisting of a "back-to-the-Bible" movement. It was the rediscovery of God's special revelation, the Epiphany experience of an enlightment. The Word of God was a new light coming in their lives to guide their paths.

Dramatically, Ezra must have strolled up to the large wooden pulpit or speakers platform erected for the occasion. The thousand gathered fixed their eyes upon him. There was a long silence as everyone held his breath and waited. Ezra slowly reached into the big sack he had carried, pulled out the large ancient scroll, blew off the dust, and began reading the Word of God to the people who seemed to be hearing it for the first time. It was as if the heavens had opened, as if a voice was coming from the clouds on top of Mount Sinai.

And that is how the spiritual reformation began — and must always begin.

Gospel Is Lost To Most Modern Persons By Indifference

You ought to try to teach a confirmation class sometime or a Bible class in college and discover the appalling ignorance people have about the Bible. Years ago I was a college professor and taught Bible. I would say to the class, "Tell me, who was Mary?" There would be a long pause and I would walk up to some young boy and say, "Hey, she was Joshua's wife, wasn't she?" "Oh, yes sir, that's who she was." Or I'd say, "No, I'm not quite sure; maybe she was the sister of Ezra?" "Yeah, that's right." I never cease to be surprised at our appalling ignorance of the Bible.

There was a minister who went to an elementary school class on visitor day, and the teacher asked if any of the guests had a question they would like to ask the class. He replied, "Yes, I've got one. I'd like to know something about their biblical background and their moral training." She said. "If you want to know something about their moral training ask a question." He said. "I'd like to know who tore down the walls of Jericho?" One little boy in the back of the room feeling guilty jumped up and said, "I didn't do it," to which the teacher said, "Listen, mister, Johnny's one of the finest, most moral boys in this classroom. If Johnny said he didn't tear them down, he didn't." The man took the problem to the principal and told him what had happened. The principal said, "Listen, mister, don't make any trouble. That is one of the best teachers I have in this school system. If she said Johnny didn't tear down the walls of Jericho, I believe her." So he thought he would take the problem to the school board. He told them the problem. They said, "Listen, this is the best principal in the school system and, if he says that his best teacher vouches for Johnny, then we don't believe he tore down the walls of Jericho. But we don't want any trouble so if you will tell us how much it cost, we will have them rebuilt." It is appalling, the ignorance people have of the Bible.

I heard about a young man who walked into the magnificent

library at Duke University, which contains miles and miles of books of every discipline, including philosophy, science, religion, literature and history. He walked up to the main desk and he asked, "Can you tell me where you keep the comic books?" Now we find it appalling that that young man had the chance to have his life revolutionized, changed, transformed, enlightened, enlarged, but was totally unaware of these possibilities around him. He was still concerned with comic books. How often this is true in our lives.

The Bible, the Gospel, really *is* buried under the sands and earth of neglect and indifference, and it might as well be in some cryptic tomb or in some cave by the Dead Sea. The novel, *The Word,* presumed that the whole world was waiting for this discovery. But there were evil forces and factors, sinister plots trying to keep the world from finding out about it. That is nothing new. For nineteen centuries you and I have had the Bible. It has been printed in 1,826 different languages. There is one in the home of practically every church member, and yet it is still a lost gospel to most of us because we have not read it and been changed by it. We have not really believed in the authenticity of it nor have you met the One about whom it speaks, who is alive and lives and brings great power to those who believe. The important point in the movie *The Word* was that you cannot ignore this gospel. The P.R. man, Steve, the main character, finally met the living Christ about whom that gospel spoke. It changed his life but he still had great doubts about the authenticity of this gospel book. So he dedicated himself to spending the rest of his life trying to disprove this book. At the end he is reconciled with his lover, Angela, the archaeologist's daughter, whose life has also now been changed by this God about whom this gospel spoke. They are reconciled. Her life has been changed, and she plans to spend the rest of her life in proving the authenticity of this particular book. Now the point is that you are never supposed to be indifferent to the gospel.

The important thing is that you meet the God about whom the Bible speaks and know him in your heart; that your life be committed to either prove or disprove the book; that you are not supposed to be indifferent to it; that you are not supposed to let it sit on your night table with two magazines on top of it and hardly ever read it. The Bible must be more than a book you infrequently open and read on special occasions. It is not supposed to be some press for flowers and photographs, to be hidden on the coffee table or to sit on the bookcase as some kind of ornament. You are not supposed to be indifferent to it because when you do, you have lost it, and you make it a lost gospel. You are supposed to react to it. But we have made it a lost gospel. So if the world would hear the message, it would sound like something new.

Studder-Kennedy, the great English poet, described that problem when he wrote the poem:

> *When Jesus came to Golgotha they*
> *   hanged Him on a tree*
> *They drove great nails through hands*
> *   and feet and made a Calvary,*
> *They crowned Him with a crown of thorns,*
> *   red were His wounds and deep.*
> *For those were crude and cruel days,*
> *   and human flesh was cheap.*
>
> *When Jesus came to Birmingham, they*
> *   simply passed Him by,*
> *They never hurt a hair of Him, they*
> *   only let Him die,*
> *For men had grown more tender, and*
> *   they would not give Him pain.*
> *They just only passed down the*
> *   street, and left Him in the rain.*
>
> *Still Jesus cried, "Forgive them for they*
> *   know not what they do,"*
> *And still it rained the winter rain and*
> *   drenched Him thru and thru,*
> *The crowds went home and left the streets*
> *   without a soul to see,*
> *And Jesus crouched against a wall and*
> *   cried for Calvary.*

Yes, you and I make it a lost gospel by our indifference to it.

II. Need to Discover and to Share It

The other point the story from Nehemiah is making is that we need to discover this gospel and, by the best means of public relations known to modern folk and mass media, to evangeliae it to the whole world. We need to unveil it to all the people! In the television movie, "The Word," you remember that the plot was to find the best public relations man and firm in the world, people who could get the press to tell the whole world that Jesus had risen from the dead and lives among us. Each evening for four evenings, the sequence began by introducing you to that dramatic scene of that famous Bible scholar who had spent his whole life searching desperately for that hidden treasure. You see the camera focusing on his making that discovery, digging it up. In those catacombs the camera focused on the searching and the digging to unearth it. And there were the flickering torches as he groped in the darkness of the cave. Then the cameras zoomed in close on the face of that man when the object of his whole life had been fulfilled. Suddenly, he found that stone crypt and container, and he pried it open and began to unwrap that ancient scroll with great tenderness and reverence. Very meticulously and delicately he unrolled it to read it. He handled it with awe. Suddenly, the room began to light up and was illuminated as he made that discovery. And each episode began with the camera focusing on that man's face, the emotion as he read for the first time the gospel and as he wiped away the tears of joy from his glasses, he realized that what he had discovered can change his life.

Each time I viewed the scene I thought of the scene of Ezra in Nehemiah 8:1-10. Now the movie was fiction but Ezra was not. This is what it should mean to all seekers who have had a Bible all their lives but one day they open it and read. For the first time they discover that good news, and it changes their life. What joy and satisfaction they will experience! It will be the answer to the questions of your life when you discover that hidden treasure. The plot of the movie was announcing that discovery to the whole world, to use the finest means of mass media and technology to make that release at one instantaneous moment, so that every human being on this earth might hear that the gospel had been found. The novel tried to emphasize the lives that had been changed. It spoke about a crippled secretary who had been healed. It talked about an alcoholic P. R. man named Steve whose life and morals had been changed. It talked about a prostitute who had found Christ. It talked about tax collectors and even preachers whose lives were drastically changed when they found the gospel. But the thing I will remember about that movie is the expression on the faces of those people who were brought into that large, well-fortified safe where they kept those documents. Inside that vault you see them as they read for the first time the gospel. They had possessed it all their lives, but they had never read it. For the first time they read it, and you see the expression on their faces as the change comes in their minds and lives.

There is a joy when you find the gospel. It will change your life. I don't know when, but I hope you will go home and take your pick and shovel and dig and unearth the Holy Scripture. That you will find and rediscover and unfold from the dust of your den or living room or shelf God's word. Unearth it from all that dust and read it with the certainty and the anticipation in your heart that you have now found that which can change the whold world. We need to get the message all over the world. We need to make that announcement: God's word has been found! It can change the world. What an announcement, what a find! Say to all people, "I've found it and it is authentic beyond all question. Just read it, believe in it, and be changed."

"And Ezra opened the book in the sight of all the people." (Nehemiah 8:5)

Jeremiah 1:4-10   *Epiphany 4 (Common, Lutheran)*
Ordinary Time 4 (Roman Catholic)

I'll Be Listening For My Name

Does God speak to you today just as he spoke to Abraham, Moses, Samuel, Isaiah, John, Jesus, and Paul? Does he speak to you the same way He spoke to them? Maybe that might not be a good question. Let me ask the question. "Does God speak to persons today just as he did those in Bible times?" The answer to that question is, "Yes!" If you say, "Well, He hasn't spoken to me like that," it is simply because you haven't listened, because he still speaks to men and women just as he did then.

H. G. Wells, who was one of the brilliant and sharp writers of his time, had a pen sharper than a two-edged sword. He wrote a short story in "The New Yorker Magazine" about an archbishop who was aging and losing his grip. His Grace no longer had the dynamic kind of decisive personality that he once had. What was worse, everyone around him began to notice that he was losing his grip. And they began to whisper about him, and he could hear their whispers. In fact, he got so concerned that he decided that he would pray to God about it. That was pretty drastic! So he approached his prayer altar and knelt down. He felt naked without his prayer book from which he had prayed for some fifty years. But he was desperate and there at his private altar he prayed, "O, God." Then he heard a voice neither friendly nor hostile but brisk that said, "Yes, what is it?" And Wells writes, "They found His Grace in the morning. He had slipped off the steps on which he had been kneeling and lay sprawling on the crimson carpet. Plainly his death had been instantaneous. Those who found him reported that the arch-bishop's face displayed, not its habitual serenity, but an extremity of terror and dismay." I dare say that some of you who have refused to listen to God's voice, if you did finally hear it, would probably drop dead, too!

You have heard the story of the fellow who fell over a mountainside on a dark night. He grabbed for anything that could break his fall. After he had fallen for some 200 yards, he grabbed a root and there he clung desperately for his life. When his energy was giving way, in desperation he cried up to the top of the mountain, "Is there anyone up there?" A voice said, "Yes." He cried back up, "Tell me what to do." The voice called down, "Turn loose." To which he called again, "Is there anyone else up there?"

Most of the time we don't acknowledge God's call, primarily because He is asking us to do something we are afraid to do. When the ground is only three feet below our feet, we are frightened of turning loose.

Jereaiah was from the little village of Anthoth. It was to this village Solomon banished David's priest Abrathar. It was around 600 B.C. The reforms of Josiah had been abandoned and their religion had deteriorated, having no king or leader who followed God. This first chapter is Jeremiah's personal testimony of how God called him. He prefaces all of this autobiographical account with his strong belief in predestination. Unlike his contemporary Isaiah, he was reluctant to answer the call and do what God was commissioning him to do. Jeremiah's reluctance was not due to the fact that he was young; that was no excuse. His reluctance was to be a prophet to *all* the nations. Like Jonah, he didn't "cotton to strangers" or regard gentiles of much value. In verse nine God says to Jeremiah that his word will be the divine energy to accomplish the task: "Behold, I will put my words in your mouth." God also assures him in verse eight, "Be not afraid of them for I am with you to deliver you." In summary, God is saying to Jeremiah: what I am calling you to do needs to be done. God promises he won't call us to do something we can't do, and he will never call us to do anything alone.

I. God Won't Ever Call Us To Do Something That Doesn't Need To Be Done

God won't ever ask us to do something that is not important. Jeremiah thought "Lord, this is a waste of time. Those gentiles are vulgar, Godless, dirty, immoral. Lord, don't you know how they treat us Hebrews? You are wasting your time." Jeremiah was a country boy who didn't like folks in the big city up north. He couldn't see any good in those people.

Everyone has had a call from God. I have had mine. God called me to do something, and I thought it not too important and so I wouldn't do it. Or I would protest, "I don't want to go to that place." Every one of you has had some place or some thing that God called you to do but you didn't want to do, or that you didn't think was important. The first three or four years following Divinity School, I wrestled with a call to do personal evangelism. God kept saying to me, "I want you to witness to people personally, eyeball to eyeball, about Jesus Christ and call them to repentance." That didn't sound too tasteful. Anyway, I rationalized that I would be judgmental if I did that. I was thinking that God wanted me to do the converting and the judging, not Him. All he wanted me to do was to be the messenger. I don't know what spiritual hurdle you have in your life that God has set before you and called you to do that you have refused. But you have your Ninevehs, like Jonah, don't you? We all do. Jeremiah did.

I think sometimes we write off a lot of persons as unimportant because we measure their value by the world's standards. I heard of a woman whose husband was missing, and she was concerned about him because she had never lived without him. So she went down to the police station to report him missing. The captain said, "Well, give me a description of him before I put out an all-points bulletin on him." She began to describe him. She said, "He is short, fat, balding, wears thick glasses, and — oh, just forget it." A lot of times we are that way. When we stop to evaluate things and take a look at them we say, "Oh, they are not too important." But God will not call you to do anything that is not important.

Many of you remember Peter Marshall. Some of you have read the book his wife wrote about him, *A Man Called Peter*. Peter used to tell again and again how God called him. As a young teenager, he was out walking on the Scottish moors. It was foggy and he was alone. Suddenly he heard a voice call, "Peter" There was a great urgency in the voice. But he said he stopped and listened and moved on another step, then heard more urgently, "Peter." He paused, stumbled, and fell to his knees and said, "Speak, Lord." As he fell he put out his hands to catch himself and found nothing there. He was on the very edge of a cliff. One more step would have been his certain death. Now Peter Marshall was sure that God called him, that God had a purpose in his life to have intervened so specifically. Obviously God was in his life, and I am sure that he was glad that he heard that call and didn't take another step until he answered it. Listen, listen, my friends. Somewhere, somebody is calling your name. Yes, God never calls us to do anything that doesn't need to be done.

II. God Never Calls Us to Do Something We Can't Do

God never calls us to do something we can't do. So let's not use that excuse any longer. Jeremiah felt that God was putting a responsibility on him that was beyond him. He couldn't go and convert all of the nations. But God wasn't asking him to convert them. God was just saying, "Take the message; I'll convert them." He thought it was an impossible demand of an over-optimistic, naive God who thinks everybody is important. He wouldn't listen.

Surely you have all heard those commercials on television that an office machine company uses to explain the importance of listening. I like the one showing the Titanic. The radio message comes, "There are icebergs; don't go." But they didn't listen. So the Titanic sank. Everyone can listen. God never asks you to do something you can't do, so develop the art of listening!

A woman and I were talking about the importance of her witnessing to her faith and she said to me, "Well, Jim, I can't do that." I said, "Why can't you do that?" She said, "Because all my friends are Christians." And I said, "Well, let us pray that God will enlarge your circle of friends." God is not going to ask you to do something you can't do. So don't use that as an excuse. Faithfulness is not an option or a luxury; it is a requirement.

One of my favorite singers is Roger Whitaker. One of his most haunting songs is entitled, "Oh, No, Not Me." You remember that one? It tells the story about a man who was on his way to catch a train. At the terminal he hears this blind man with a mandolin playing this song, "Oh, No, Not Me." He stops and listens. Nobody else seemed to be paying the blind man any attention. But he listens and listens. And he comes back on several other occasions just to listen to him. He feels as though that song was especially for him. And then one day the old musician dies. No one ever notices he is gone. Now the man is burdened with the fact that he is the only one in the whole world who has really heard this song. So he must respond to it. "Oh, No, Not me" he sings. "There is none so blind as those who will not see. Oh, No, Not me. The only one to hear the song was me."

Jeremiah heard the call of God and responded, "Oh, no, not me, Lord." We may hear the same call and respond the same way. But the call is like the haunting refrain of that song. It will not let go of us. We cannot escape it. "The only one who heard that song was me." You don't have to convert or convince. You just have to carry the message. So God won't ask you to do something that is not important. He won't ask you to do something you can't do.

III. God Will Never Call Us to Do Anything Alone

God will never ask us to do anything alone. He will never send us out alone to do something. He wasn't sending Jeremiah out there all by himself. He was going to prepare the hearts of the people of the nations to hear the message, as He did. You know, every time I fail to remember that whatever I do I don't do alone, I fail at it. Every time I fail to remember that when I preach I don't preach alone, I fail at preaching. It is that way with all of us. God told Moses to go and lead the children out of the land of Egypt. "Just tell the Pharoah; I'll take care of the rest. And I'll be with you even unto the ends of the earth. You won't go alone."

We need to get outside ourselves and to hear God's call. To hear God calling gives you a feeling of security, doesn't it? An identification. It makes you feel like somebody. Have you ever been to a meeting, particularly when you were a teenager or a child, and they called the whole list of people who were supposed to be there or called out the people who made the team and you hoped they would call your name? You sat there nervous and frightened that they might not call your name. The fact that your name was called meant that you were somebody and made you feel you belonged and were not alone.

Descartes, the famous philosopher, said that we prove our existence by thinking. "I think, therefore I am," says Descartes. But the Bible says, "I hear God call and respond; therefore I am." That is how I know I am somebody because God calls my name. That makes me somebody. The Bible says, "I hear God calling my name." In the second chapter of Genesis it speaks of God walking through the garden calling us, and our trying to run away and hide from Him in the Garden of Eden. He cries out, "Adam, Adam where are you?" We don't answer, but he calls. He says, "You will never be asked to do anything alone. I will be with you."

I've been with a lot af families when they went through cardiac surgery. Duke Hospital has one nurse assigned to just one patient. And she comes in the day before the operation and to all patients, adults and child alike, she says, "I want you to hold my hand. I want you to get the feel of my hand. I want you to hold my hand a lot today, because tomorrow after surgery when you wake up in ICU, you will be unable to see a thing and for several hours you will be almost paralyzed. You won't be able to know if anyone else is there except by the touch of my hand. I want you to get the feel of it and recognize it, so that when you awaken tomorrow you won't be frightened. You'll know someone is with you, that I have got your hand in mine." I have talked to patient after patient who has been through cardiac surgery at the great hospitals. They all say that a person being there holding their hand really made a big difference, to know that whatever you are going through, that you are not alone. Yes, God calls you.

My favorite gospel hymn is that old spiritual: "When He calls me I will answer; I'll be somewhere listening for my name." Yes, as God calls each one of you, I pray that you will hear him and go and do what he wants you to do with your life.

Isaiah 6:1-8 (9-13)   Epiphany 5 (Common, Lutheran)
                         Ordinary Time 5 (Roman Catholic)

The Moment of Decision

Dr. William James, the father and founder of American psychology and a great Christian, has said that the only irrefutable thing is a religious experience. In other words, the only thing that you cannot disprove is a religious experience. Using deductive logic you can say, "All truth is based upon an experience." That is the only irrefutable truth of reality. More succinctly, Jesus simply said, "I am the truth." You can not reduce it any more simply than that. Jesus is saying that to experience him personally is to know truth. The validity and the proof of all truth and reality lies in whether or not you have had that experience.

For example, I do not remember much about my freshman year in college except my first visit home. Everyone can remember that. You were now a "college man" and it was your sworn duty to return home and impress all the ignorant folk in your little town about how smart you were and demonstrate how much college had changed you. I will never forget what I wore for that first visit. I was "decked out" with white bucks, a navy blue double-breasted suit, a knit tie, and a beanie cap. Immediately upon entering the house my Dad asked me whether I was learning anything. Apparently it did not look like I was. Trying to validate myself and having read a little bit of Tillich and Niebuhr, as well as Kierkegaard, I replied with a superficial pseudo-sophisticated South Carolina pantomime of an Oxford English accent, "The confrontation and cross-fertilization of ideas has made me cognizant of my ultimate concern in the midst of my existential despair which threatens the ground of my being." To which my Dad responded, even more confused than I was, "Ain't they taught you nothing up there?" But in spite of the fact that my vocabulary revealed or gave away my ignorance, my Dad should have spotted that I had learned that all truth and knowledge and facts had to be based on an experience. My "putting on airs" was to validate that I had had the experience in hopes he would be convinced of what I knew.

For centuries people have said that the only way you learn is by experience. I have heard that all my life. Plato based his whole philosophy on that theory. John Dewey and Thorndike in the early twentieth century built a new discipline we call education upon that theory. For example, everyone who speaks at an evangelistic meeting will inevitably give you their testimony; *then* they will get around to preaching and telling you the facts they want to "lay on you." There is a universal awareness that without a worship experience, what one says, learns, teaches, prophesies about, cannot be authenticated.

Have you ever been to an Alcoholics Anonymous meeting? That is how they do it. Have you ever been to a CFO meeting? That is how they do it. Have you ever been to an Ashram? That is how they do it. Have you ever been to a Full Gospel meeting? That is how they do it. Have you ever been to a Faith and Works meeting? That is how they do it. No speaker ever has the gall to try to share with you some truth they know, unless they can first validate the fact that it is based on an experience they have had.

Every scholarly lecturer does the same thing. No matter what the subject of their lecture, they do this. They may have three Ph.D.'s and be from the ivory towers of Harvard, but every lecturer I have ever heard from Duke to Yale has always begun just like they begin in a Full Gospel or an evangelistic meeting — by sharing with the audience their testimony of how they experienced this information or knowledge. They give a testimony of how they have gone through the process of pilgrimage, what effect it had on them and what they think. Then they get around to presenting the facts they want to present because they feel that they have thereby authenticated their right to teach you some truth.

This is true of everything in life. Athletes will tell you how, after years and years of practice, it finally clicked. Suddenly, I could hit that forehand like it ought to be hit. It finally came to me. Or we say, "For the first time in my life I saw what I was doing wrong." Then they tell you how they learned how to hit it. Or we say, "It came to me out of the blue." Or, as scholars and college students say, "Finally the truth hit me." "It was like a light turning on." "Suddenly after all those years I could do it."

Now, in matters of love it is the same way. People will tell you how, all of a sudden, they realized they were in love. "It was love at first sight." Or, "I was just swept off my feet!" Or, "The stars began shooting and sirens started going off."

Now we do that in everything, because we know that until you can substantiate the fact that you had the experience, all the facts that you are going offer anybody have no credence and no authenticity. That is what Isaiah learned. He was the prime minister of his country. Since Uzziah the great King had leprosy most of his reigning life and, since his son Ahab was not too smart, Isaiah had run the Kingdom. The problem was that King Uzziah died and Ahab had full control, and the country was going to pot. It was somewhere around 742 B.C. Ahab was now the King and he did not want to let Isaiah have much influence. Ahab was married to Jezebel who did not "cotton" to these Southern Baptist preachers in Judah and especially the Methodists.

Notice, in the first five chapters Isaiah starts trying to tell the people some brilliant ideas and observations he has about some of the peace treaties they have made and some of the things that his Congress had done. He tries to tell them that these peace treaties they have made with all these various nations in the Middle East, are not worth the paper they are written on "because we do not have our act together back home." He tells how they have sinned. He tells them that their only hope is that a Messiah will come, but they are still not listening. After about fifteen minutes into the sermon Isaiah realizes that he has not validated his prophecy, so he says, "Before we can go any further I have to validate my right to speak to you. Let me tell you about my experience. Let me tell you how I finally came to this theory."

So he tells about his experience in the Temple, saying that the truth of everything he is saying is based on that. He recalls, "It was in the year that King Uzziah died and I went, not out on the golf course, not out on a beautiful lake fishing, but to the Temple. And I saw the Lord high and lifted up. I saw the greatness of God. I heard choirs singing, 'Holy, Holy, Holy is the Lord God of hosts.' It was so overwhelming that the seraphim had to cover their eyes and their feet. After I had seen his greatness I began to see myself in comparison to the goodness of God and I said, 'I am a sinner. I am a man of unclean lips and dwell in the midst of people with unclean lips. I live in a sinful, evil world and I am a part of it.' Suddenly God pardoned me and took the coals from the altar and cleansed my sin, seared it with the fire which sterilizes it of all the contagion of sin, and said, 'You are forgiven.' " Now Isaiah's experience did not end there.

The worship service came to a close and God gave an invitation. He always does that. He gave an invitation and he said, "Who can I send?" Isaiah looked around and thought, "Who are you talking to, Lord, that guy in the forty-third row?" And Isaiah looked around again and really wondered who God was talking to. Finally he realized he was the only one in the church. God had to be talking to Isaiah. He discovered that every worship experience prevents you from going out of the door until you have had a confrontation or at least been given an invitation to make a decision, yes or no. You cannot say, "Well, maybe." Or, "I will think about it." No, every worship experience ends with a confrontation between you and God. "Who can I send?" Finally Isaiah said, "Here am I, Lord, send me" . . . the decision, the eternal "Yes." Now let's see what Isaiah experienced.

I. He Saw the Value of God

The Scripture says he saw the value of God. That is what all worship ought to accomplish. It causes you to want to adore him. Every worship ought to begin with adoring him: "How Great Thou Art" or "Holy, Holy, Holy" or "Come, Thou Fount of Every Blessing." We should begin every Sunday in church with a hymn of adoration. Some churches begin with applauding. I think that is most appropriate, applauding the greatness of God, waiting with anticipation." And I saw the Lord high and lifted up." "Holy, Holy, Holy is the Lord God of Hosts." The Lord's Prayer begins that way, and that is the perfect example of worship. You identify God: "Our Father who art in Heaven." What comes next? Adoration: "Hallowed be Thy Name." That is how we begin in celebrating the goodness of God. Once you have experienced God's greatness, love, and perfection, it causes you to then measure yourself and see how you stack up.

II. He Saw the Condition of Himself and His World

Then he saw the condition of himself and his world. He cried out, "Woe is me for I am a man of unclean lips and dwell amidst people with unclean lips." You have not worshipped if you have not, honestly and personally, X-rayed your soul, your subconsciousness and your mind. Every theologian from the liberal to the conservative has always said that is the point of beginning for Christianity: to see your predicament, your condition. It is not easy to do. is it?

I said to one of my sons one day, "Why do you do such-and such or why do you react such-and-such a way?" He said, "Daddy, where do you think I learned it?" I had a man with whom I was in counsel who was an alcoholic. He would not admit he was an alcoholic. His wife and I tried to help him see his condition. He would do things when he was drinking that he did not even know he was doing. He would not admit it until one night he heard his little son in the bed, crying out in the middle of the night, "Daddy, don't hit me again, please." For the first time he honestly saw himself. There are the sins of temperament, bitterness, resentment, anger, moodiness, and superiority. Then there are the social sins we need to confess. I am a part of society. I belong to this church. I belong to this state, this nation, this world. And its sins are part of my sins. I dwell among the people of unclean lips, too. It is complicated, I know, but you must confess that you are a part of it.

One of my favorite books is John Steinbeck's *Grapes of Wrath*. Do you remember when the old farmer's farm was being taken from him during the Depression? He was determined to go and shoot whoever was reclaiming his farm. So he took his shotgun and went to the bank and poked it right in the manager's face. The manager said, "It is not me. It is the president." So he went to the president who said, "Oh, no. it is not me; it is the Board of Directors." And he went to the Board of Directors. There were thirty-six of them and he only had two shells, but they said, "It is not us; it is the stockholders." And, for the first time in that simple man's life, he realized how complex and how social sin is and that he was also a part of it.

There are the sins of neglect, too. Do you see those? The good you should have done but did not do? That is what the parable of the Good Samaritan is about, those who passed by and went on the other side of the road because they were too busy. They neglected him.

Then there are most of us who just do not like to see ourselves honestly as we are. One of the greatest plays on Broadway was "Death of a Salesman." It starred Willy Loman, a big bag of wind, a hotshot salesman who liked to pretend that he was influential and important. He was not. Finally he could not face who he was and he killed himself. After the funeral service, his son and his wife were in the kitchen, and the son said to the mother, "You know, he never knew who he was." He had never stood in the Temple and seen himself in comparison to God. Socrates said, "Know thyself." That is imperative. And if you have seen God, you will feel the necessity to see yourself.

III. He Accepted the Pardon and Forgiveness of God

Having confessed, Isaiah accepted the pardon and the forgiveness of God. It is not enough just to admit that you have sinned, but we have to *accept* it. That is not so easy. "Behold the coals touched my lips and my guilt was taken away and my sins forgiven."

Herb Gardner wrote a beautiful story about a nonconformist kind of fellow. He was a good man, but he could not hold down a job. He had a little nephew that he reared and they did not have any specific rules. He was a colorful, lovable man, but he lacked reality. He was supposed to go down to apply for a job one day. Instead of applying for a job, he went up and down Fifty-first Street saying to everybody he saw, "Forgive me. I'm sorry." And everyone who saw him would pat him on the head and say, "You're forgiven; it's okay, buddy. Don't sweat it, man." One man hollered out of a cab, "You're forgiven." Another lady carrying her puppy dog said, "Poof forgives you."

Now forgiveness is something we all know we need, so we are willing to give it. But the problem was that this man was not aware that he had sinned and that he really needed it. He just wanted to test people's willingness to forgive. What a tragedy! Most of us are like him, running down the street asking for forgiveness when deep down we don't really believe we need it. Forgiveness is designed to put us back in good terms with God. It is to wipe away our sin. It is to receive it and let God give it to you.

IV. Call and Commitment

Isaiah's worship experience ended with a call and a commitment. "And I heard a voice from heaven saying to me, 'Whom will I send?' " Every worship service must end with an invitation, a chance for a commitment, a chance for a decision. How are you going to respond to this God whom you have just experienced? What are you going to do now that you have had your sins washed away? My friends, it is not a special call. We preachers have distorted the Scriptures so that you think a "call" is something unique. We are not special. God calls everyone who experiences him. He calls you and everyone. "Whom can I send?" That is a part of worship. Then you have to decide what you are going to do about it. Worship always ends with the experience you have just had, causing you to make ethical and moral decisions about your life.

In the Bible every experience was like that. How about Moses and the burning bush on Mount Sinai? Suddenly he was impressed by God's greatness and the bush was aflame, beautiful and magnificent, and he knew he was in the presence of holiness. He took off his shoes and fell to his knees and cried. "Forgive me." And he went through the whole process of dialogue and experiencing of God in such a magnificent fashion there. It ended with what? "Go down into the valley where the people are; do not stay up here on this mountain. Go down and serve and love and help." Always it ends that way. That is why we always have an invitation at every worship service to which we can respond.

Dag Hammerskjold, who was Executive Secretary of the United Nations and was killed, was a deeply spiritual man. In his autobiography he wrote in one sentence a description of his religious experience: "A moment in which I said yes; after that, I could not look back." The same words of the text we have from Paul today say. "Behold, all things will become new and the old will pass away."

Notice that even after Jesus at age twelve went to the Temple, what happened? How did He respond? Immediately, at the end of the worship, He began the service when He said, "Did you not know that I must now be about my Father's business?"

In every biography I have ever read about great men and women, they have all spoken of a moment, a moment in which they made a decision that changed and altered their lives. And I listen to the testimony of lesser men and women often, who tell me about that moment in which they almost decided, but they did not. Every one of you who has worshiped has heard a call, "Who will go?" Or, "Will you go?" Yes or no? You must answer.

It is the moment of decision right now.

Jeremiah 17:5-10 *Epiphany 6 (Common, Lutheran)*
Ordinary Time 6 (Roman Catholic)

The Coming of Jesus Illuminates Humanity

During the Advent and Christmas season we have emphasized a good deal the incarnation, that God became human which event glorifies "flesh" and our humanity. Now we are hit with this Epiphany lesson from Jeremiah 17:5-10, which strikes at trusting in humanity and humanism. However, we should not jump to any conclusions or get on the defensive until we have examined this passage.

We need to recognize that this is a poem of contrast. It is a contrast between those who trust in self and those who trust in God. In verse five Jeremiah says, "Cursed is the man who trusts in man." Jeremiah likens such a person to a shrub trying to live in a desert with no soil or moisture to feed and nourish it. In verse seven is the contrast: "Blessed is the man who trusts in the Lord." He likens this person to a tree planted by water with deep roots in good moist soil. In verse ten, he explains that our worth lies in the fact that God cares for him: "I the Lord search the mind and try the heart, to give to every man according to his ways, according to the fruit of his doing." This is affirmed by saying God searches each individual mind and tries the heart, judging us by what degree we trust God or self. This emphatically denies universal salvation, which is the weakness of much of today's humanism.

Let me tell you honestly that I approached this sermon with fear and trembling. Yet, I think the word of God needs to be spoken regarding a case for or against "Humanism." Let me share with you something of my background. Like many of you, I was schooled in a classical, liberal arts education in which I studied Dewey, Emerson, Thorndyke, Locke, Hegel, Spinoza, Hume, Rousseau and all the other humanists. Judging them on the criteria of their reasonableness and their brilliance, they made good sense. But you must understand that I read them, as most of you read them, from my Christian background. I was presuming that the prerequisite of all of this was the Christian faith. Let me say that most of these philosophers wrote their humanism presuming it to operate within a culture that was Christ-centered historically.

Now the problem has been that, in our times, people have read these humanistic thoughts without the context of a Christian background and without any assumption that Christianity is presumed. What happens, of course, is that when you deal with humanism without the background and the foundation of the Christian gospel, you produce frustratian and despair. You produce something that is totally inadequate and that inevitably evolves into an atheistic humanism like Marxism, Moaism, Secularism and Communism. Our age, as one French philosopher said, "is an age that is concerned — no, not just concerned; it has an *obsession* — with man."

A French biologist has defined modern humanism with a good analogy. He said, "There was a man who discovered he had a shadow. Watching its lithe motion, he assumed that the shadow was alive because it followed him faithfully. He then decided it must be his servant, but gradually he began to believe he was imitating the shadow. He took increasing time and care for the comfort and welfare of his shadow. In fact, when he would sit or lie down, he would take great precaution to make sure he got his shadow exactly in the right place in the chair or bed. He awkwardly maneuvered everything in that direction, but eventually the man became, in effect, the shadow of a shadow. This is the weakness of modern-day shallow humanism, read from the twentieth century perspective which has no presumption of a Christian background.

You can look at it historically. Our century could be seen as a drama in two acts. The first act was primarily a confident expectation of the good and the potentiality of humankind. It was assumed that humanity was getting better and better until, ultimately, it would reach perfection. But the Second World War came along and, suddenly, we had to face the horror of humanity's capability for cruelty and evil. Suddenly we became disillusioned with humanity. God was not included in this first act.

In the 1950s we began this century's second act. This was an effort to take a more realistic look at the dignity of humanity. But the problem is we are having to do it amidst the dehumanization of institutions, growing technology, and computerization. This, too, is a humanism without God. But there has been more "humanism" among what we call Bible-thumping, Bible-believing literalists than anybody else.

As a boy I saw it in the culture in which I grew up. Good men, who were active in the church, would say that all you needed to believe was the Golden Rule, "Do unto others as you would have them do unto you." That, they said, was Christianity in a nutshell. Even as a boy, I wanted to scream out, "That is heresy!" That is presuming goodness measured by how I react to my fellows without a relationship with God. So we can't suggest that the so-called liberal philosophers and educators are the only atheistic humanists of our time. It has been an integral part of every one of us.

I have heard hundreds of evangelical preachers on TV and radio argue that humanism is the greatest threat that Christianity has to face. These members of the theological conservative God-squad mobilize themselves for a war against humanistic philosophy, which they believe is rearing its ugly head everywhere. They call humanism the "Gog" or Satan come down from the North, as outlined in Revelation. Fundamentalists have built colleges and high schools, knowing that is one way you can raise money. They believe that humanism is threatening us, and the only way we can escape it is by sending our children to a "Christian school." They build church buildings from the income of the student tuitions. They can build education buildings for the church without the church putting any investment into it. They have frightened people until they have become paranoid, looking for humanists under every bush. Let me tell you emphatically that neither the fundamentalists nor the liberal philosophers have a very good definition of humanism.

With all the noise and fury that goes on from both sides, I realize that it is hard to say anything positive about humankind without being misunderstood. But God has laid this on my heart to say: I think that the gospel is about being human. I think that Jesus came into the world primarily to deliver us from the dehumanizing behaviors and tendencies of society and to make us into human beings as he willed us to be when He created us. I think that being saved means realizing our potential for humanness rather than becoming or trying to escape an evil world. In short, I believe that Christianity is about achieving humanity and building on the premise that true humanness can only come through an intimate relationship with Jesus Christ. So I decided, with God's pushing, that He and I would preach this sermon. I am going to bypass what Ralph Waldo Emerson, Dewey or Hegel or any other brilliant philosopher has said. I am going to ignore the pronouncements of the moral majority or Jerry Falwell. What I want to do is open the Bible and share with you what it says about humanism in Jeremiah 17:5-10.

A professor who teaches at an Ivy League school recorded this: "It was late one Thursday afternoon in a seminar, at a time when all the students were drowsy and just waiting for the bell. I asked them what they wanted out of life. Immediately this sociology class came alive. One boy said, 'I want to become human, fully human.' Then he stood up, which was unusual behavior in this kind of informal setting. 'We all want to be human', he said. 'We don't know how to be human and nothing I've heard in this class up to this point has provided any hints.' That is a good question. Let's presume that young man's question is the question of every human being or every being. How can I become fully human?"

I. Our Infinity is with our Maker, not the Made

Our infinity, that with which we should compare ourselves, is with our Maker, *not* things made. The Psalmist wrote, "When I consider the heavens, the works of thy hand, the sun, the moon and the stars and all thou hast made, what is man that thou art mindful of him? What is the Son of Man that thou carest for him?" But don't compare humanity to the sun, the moon and the stars and the heavens, for God has made us like God, "a little lower than the angels." Don't compare yourself to creation. If you do, there is frustration, despair, failure, and defeat. I am not supposed to compare myself to a computer. I can't do a lot of things a computer can do. Nor am I supposed to compare myself to a sun or moon, there is no pattern for humanity there. Rather, I am supposed to compare myself to God.

To compare ourselves to creation is to become disillusioned. For example, the sociologists list four points of dehumanization in modern times. The first is *the expendability of man*. That dehumanizes. Well, if I compare myself to a napkin, a computer, or an automobile, then I am expendable. Everything is disposable in our society. But compare yourself to God, who is not expendable. The second dehumanization is *changed meaning of work.* Today we feel as though we are part of an assembly line with no purpose. If all I am supposed to do is draw a check, rather than glorify God, then I am dehumanized. The third point is *the technological revolution.* If I compare myself to a robot on the assembly line, and if the robot can weld faster than I can weld, I am going to come up short. Finally, the fourth dehumanization is *regarding a human as a thing instead of a person.* If I see myself only as a number, when I go to the bank or to the social security office, then I am not a person, but a thing! I am not merely a statistic; I compare myself to God because my infinity is with my Maker, not what is made.

All dehumanization is caused by comparing self to something made, even another person. "I might be bad, but I'm not as bad as so and so." If you keep comparing yourself to anything that is made, rather than God, you are going to become disenchanted and you are going to be dehumanized. People say, "I need to get in touch with myself." The only way you are going to get in touch with yourself is by getting in touch with God and especially God in human form as revealed in Jesus.

When I discover God in Jesus, who became a man, I discover not only God, but I discover my humanness. So to discover divinity, I have got to discover humanness. When I discover divinity, I have discovered humanness. Only in Jesus was there ever a perfect person.

II. Our Human Worth Is That God Cares For Us

Our human worth is not that we are human, but that God cares for us. My worth is not that I was made by God or that I am a human being. No, what makes me of value is that God cares for me individually. He thinks about trees, but he thinks about all the trees in the world. He thinks about tomatoes, but He thinks about all the tomatoes. Jeremiah says "that humankind uniquely is thought about by God; he searches my mind and my heart." That is my glory, not whether I succeed by automation standards of the computerized world in which I live, but that "God loves me and has crowned me then with glory and honor because I am loved and known by him."

III. We Only Discover Our True Humanity by Trusting in and Knowing God

We only discover our true humanity by discovering Jesus. I don't watch a lot of television, but for some strange reason I was watching "St. Elsewhere" last week. One of the patients in a psychiatric ward was a brilliant man who thought he was a bird. He even ate birdseed and worms. He had never seen clearly any example of humanity, so in his frustration, he had become a bird. Finally, he decided he was going to become himself. But the problem was that, within himself, was not a perfect example of humanity. He had no role model, no prototype. He looked into himself and at the end of the show, he dove off the roof of the hospital, clinging to his illusion rather than his reality. It was easy for him to believe he was a bird. But to become a human was difficult, because he didn't know what a human was supposed to be like.

Eugene O'Neill said the same thing almost fifty years ago in his play, "Long Day's Journey into the Night". Edmond looked about at his mother and brother, who were drug addicts, and his father who was an alcoholic. They were his only models of humanity and he says, "You know, it would have better had I been born a seagull." We are frustrated when we look to anything but Jesus for an example of our humanity.

Let us return to the conversation in the Ivy League classroom. The young man has just said, "I want to be human. We all want to be human, but we don't know how to be." The professor says, "What do you mean by human? Can you describe the traits of humanness? Can you list the characteristics of humanness?"

The boy answered, "It means to be loving, infinitely loving, sensitive, infinitely sensitive, aware, totally aware, empathetic, completely empathetic, forgiving, graciously forgiving. I could go on but I would only be elaborating on the obvious. Everyone in here knows what I am talking about when I say humanness. You do, too, so stop putting me on." "Okay," the professor said, "I was putting you on. I do know what you mean by humanness. But I must probe a bit further. You know something of love, not a lot, but you know something of love; you know something of empathy and you have a little forgiveness in you. Even you possess these traits to a limited degree. You obtained them somewhere and somehow. Were you born with them? Were they built into your biological structure? How did they come about?"

"Oh, you're putting me on again," said the student, "This is a sociology class and you are a sociologist, and you know whatever qualities of humanness I possess are obtained oy the process of socialization. If I am forgiving, it is because I associated with forgiving people and took on their traits and likenesses. If I possess a sense of awareness to life, it is only because I interacted with people who lived in this way. If there is any love in me, it is because I have been loved by others. You know all that, so stop trying to put me on."

The professor said, "What I am trying to do is to drive you back to a simple definition of socialization which you learned in the introductory class of sociology. Do you remember what it said? Socialization is the process whereby a homo sapiens becomes human. We taught you that if, at the moment of birth, you were separated from all human beings and raised by wolves in a forest, twenty years later you would possess none of these traits you have so eloquently suggested are evidence of humanness. All the traits that you listed in your attempt to describe humanness would be lacking. You would not even have a consciousness of self, for, without social relationships, you would never develop the reflective capacities that are essential for self-awareness. It is only by adopting the perspective of a significant other that you become conscious that you are an existing person. In short, without interaction with human beings you would have the form of a man, but none of the traits." The professor continued, "What I'm trying to tell you is that the traits of humanness are gained by associating with someone who possesses them. If you have an intimate and sustaining interactive relationship with somebody who is very loving, you will become loving too."

Finally, the boy said, "Yes. I know that, but you don't understand. If I want to be fully human, want to be a total actualized person as Abraham Maslow describes it, if I am to become everything that I potentially am, I must have a relationship with somebody like that. *And I don't know anybody like that!* If I only become as human as the most significant person I relate to, then I can never become fully human, because there is no one I can relate to who has achieved this status. In fact, you say society is supposed to socialize me. I feel as though society is dehumanizing me at every turn." The professor writes, "It was a perfect set-up. I knew it and he knew it." I said, "Yes, that is the problem but there is a person like that."

"His name is Jesus. Read the New Testament. Read it honestly and openly. Read the gospels specifically. Learn about Jesus and as you learn about him, ask a very simple question: doesn't Jesus possess the fullness of humanity? He is the only person who has ever lived who was perfectly human. No cynic or skeptic has ever been able to attack the fact that 'He was perfect'. Isn't He infinitely loving, graciously forgiving, totally empathetic, infinitely aware of people in the world in which he lives? Well, you might ask 'How can this guy who lived two thousand years ago help my humanization or my relationship here now?' You know the answer because we know that this Jesus was raised from the dead and is alive and present among us, lives among us. You can know him. You can have that kind of relationship with him. He was the only perfect man and I can relate in him and I can become like him."

And only as I become like him can I become a real human being. For socialization of society dehumanized me. Only Jesus humanizes me. Wouldn't you like to be fully human? You can. Jeremiah says, "Blessed is the man who trusts in the Lord for he will give to every man according to his ways, according to the fruits of his doings."

Genesis 45:3-11, 15 *Epiphany 7 (Common, Lutheran)*
Ordinary Time 7 (Roman Catholic)

Recognizing God in Our Midst

H. G. Wells, in his book *The Soul of a Bishop,* relates a conversation between an angel and the bishop who asks to be told the "truth". Placing his hand on the bishop's bald head, the angel asks, "Could this hold it?" Perhaps we should go a step further and ask, "Would we recognize it?"

Mankind has always had problems seeing God and comprehending his presence. God has always had the problem of revealing himself to humankind in a way that we could comprehend him and recognize him. The incarnation, "God becoming human", was God's answer to his problem and our answer to his problem. God "took on the form of man," and "the Word became flesh and dwelt among us."

This story from Genesis about Joseph who became ruler of the world in his day was a prototype of what would take place with the revealing of God in the Messiah. Though he lived in their midst in Canaan, Joseph's family, did not recognize his greatness; neither did they recognize his human identity when they saw him as the ruler of Egypt. They failed to recognize that Joseph was the remnant of Israel which would enable them to live on and who would save them from death and oblivion. But, let us examine more closely this Epiphany text.

We humans have two serious difficulties:

I. Recognizing God In Our Midst

In the story of Cinderella every child is taught how even the meek and ignored person may be transformed into a person of importance who can save the whole family from oblivion and poverty. "Cinderella" shows how the meek and lowly can be elevated to royalty and importance. Cinderella's stepmother and stepsisters could not recognize her identity at the royal palace nor in the royal coach. The point of the story is that a servant girl was in their midst, looking like a beautiful princess, and they did not recognize her. Often we do not recognize greatness and royalty even when it is among us.

We have a similar story in Genesis 45:3-11, concerning Joseph. It is the last part of one of the greatest dramas, one of the greatest "rags-to-riches" stories recorded in history. Recall: Joseph was the most complete prototype of Christ in all the Bible. Joseph and Jesus had the following similarities:

1. No word or reproof against them.
2. Favored son.
3. Rejected by family and brothers.
4. Severely tempted but resisted.
5. Taken to Egypt.
6. Sold for price of a slave.
7. Unjustly accused.
8. Exalted a ruler after suffering.
9. Called "Remnant of Israel".
10. Sent to save and preserve life.

Note that Jesus, like Joseph, "came unto his own but his own received him not." His brothers rejected his dreams and mission. In fact, they thought him "beside himself."

Joseph, rejected by his brothers, is sold to foreigners. He is unjustly accused and placed in solitary confinement in a maximum security prison. He is exalted, in a matter of minutes, from the dungeon to royalty and ruler of the world. The famine brought his brothers from Canaan to acquire food for survival. They recognized the power and importance of Joseph as a mighty ruler and feared him, but they did not recognize him as Joseph their brother. They recognized his kingship, but not his humanity nor his kinship to them. Remember that back in Canaan they had not recognized the royalty in this brother named Joseph. The point of the story is that, had Joseph not revealed and disclosed himself and his identity to them, they would never have recognized his true identity. Karl Barth taught, "By God alone can God be known."

For Epiphany this is perhaps the most appropriate Scripture in the Old Testament. For Epiphany is to teach us that God always has to disclose himself; otherwise we would never recognize or know him. This Epiphany lesson reminds us that God our King is revealed to his half brothers (gentiles) as well as to his whole brother Benjamin (the Jew).

Kings, by nature, ruled from their thrones, hidden behind their motes. They were regarded as divine, not human and unaware of the problems of life that inflict mortals. Mere humans did not feel kinship with kings of rulers. I love the old story of the young king who left his throne to live incognito among his common subjects, believing that, if he were to rule them and save them, he must be in their midst. That is the meaning of "Emmanuel": "God is with and among us." Wesley said it best in his hymn "Veiled in flesh and Godhead see." "So Joseph said to his brothers, Come near to me, I am your brother Joseph."

II. Recognizing Our Remnant and Savior

Our other difficulty is recognizing that Jesus is our Savior. In verse eleven Joseph says, "I will provide for you" and in verse five he says "God sent me before you to preserve life." His power, royalty and might is for the one purpose of carrying out God's plan to save us and provide for us.

Joseph's brothers were afraid of Joseph and thought he intended to harm them and punish them. They could not conceive that he intended only good for them; that He would save, not destroy them; and that he would provide for them, not take away.

Back in Canaan, Israel and his children were living on the edge of disaster and extinction. Joseph's brothers had made their last desperate attempt and had failed. Now they were prisoners of a foreign king. The loss of Joseph and now Benjamin would bring final despair to their father Israel. Without hope that a Savior would yet come, without hope that God would provide a small remnant to continue Israel, there was only despair. This story demonstrates how God provides a remnant (verse seven) and a means of solution, so that we need never give up hope. When there seems to be no way out, God acts. This hope is what will keep Israel going and his "remnant" alive. According to the Bible, pessimism is another name for atheism. The dictionary gives pessimism the same definition. If you are a pessimist, it is because you have ignored God's plan to save us and provide for us.

In 2 Kings appears the story of Elijah's servant who looked over the city walls and, seeing the enemy, came to Elijah saying there was no hope, only despair. Elijah fell to his knees and prayed, "O Lord, God, open the eyes of my servant." God opened his eyes and he looked over the wall again and now he saw the valleys and hills encircled by the chariots and horses of the Almighty God. There is a difference in the eyes through which we see, whether eyes of faith or eyes of despair. The "remnant" mentioned in this seventh verse is explained also in the Old Testament hope that out of the root of Israel and Jesse his descendant will come forth the great ruler and savior.

Several years ago, a retired judge gave me some ugly old roots in a burlap sack. I threw them in the garage where they remained all winter and all the next year. In the spring, with little faith, I dug some holes and put them in the ground. That summer, my home was encircled with the most beautiful calla lilies I had ever seen. When there seems to be no hope from an old snarled, chopped up root, there will spring forth life and joy.

And Joseph said, "God sent me before you to preserve you a remnant on earth, and to keep alive for you many survivors." (Genesis 45:7) May we recognize God in our midst and find that He is our hope.

Isaiah 55:10-13

Epiphany 8 (Common, Lutheran)
Ordinary Time 8 (Roman Catholic)

Prayer: How to be Sure of Results

Recently a newspaper ran a list of thirteen possible sermon topics and asked the readers to select the one on which they would most like to hear their pastor preach. There were only a few over 7,000 replies and 7,000 of them replied that the subject on which they would like their minister to preach would be "How to Make Prayer More Effective." The Bible tells us that this was the only request that the disciples made of Jesus. When they had to select among all the subjects upon which they would want him to speak, their only request was "Lord, teach us how to pray." That sounds a little ridiculous, since it comes from the disciples whom he had selected because they were good and religious men who had probably prayed all their lives in some fashion or another. Yet they wanted to know how to pray. That question comes not from the heathen but from the righteous. They did not ask Jesus to teach them how to pray in response to a powerful, moving sermon that he had preached on prayer. It was not the result of some clever, philosophical argument for the cause and effectiveness of prayer; nor was it as a result of some lectures He had given on the need and technique of prayer.

The Bible says that the disciples asked him to teach them how to pray because they saw in his life power and change that was wrought as a result of prayer. St. Luke writes that it came to pass that, as he was praying, one of the disciples came up to Jesus and said, "Lord, teach us how to pray. Preach a sermon on how to pray." They requested this because they had noticed that when he returned after going away to pray, there was something different about his life. There was a different countenance and attitude about him. They saw the effectiveness of it in his life. It was so obvious that they asked him, "Lord, teach us how to pray." They reasoned, "If it can do *that* for him, think what it could do for *us!* Maybe we are not praying in the proper manner." This passage struck me because, in a moment of honesty, I admitted that it really was a judgment of my own prayer life. How many times had church members asked me to teach them how to pray? And I had to be honest with myself. Perhaps the reason I had not been asked to teach praying was because my own prayer life was not effective enough that it made my congregation want to learn more about how to pray. In that rare moment of honesty, I evaluated the poverty of my own prayer life.

Everything you read says that people are praying less today than ever before. They wonder in the scientifically-explained world how prayer could have any effect. We have scientific explanations for almost everything. Surveys taken in the last few years, among church members and especially among clergy, show that they are praying less, and they feel guilty about it and have questions about its effectiveness in their own life. I want to talk to people like myself who, from time to time, have questions about the effectiveness of their prayer life. I do not want to give you any glib answers, but I do want to tell you how Jesus said that you can have 100 percent success in your prayer life — not 99 percent but 100 percent. You can always be sure, if you approach it this way, that it will work all the time.

I would like to call your attention to the passage from the fifty-fifth chapter of the Prophet Isaiah in which he is addressing the Hebrew children who find themselves in Babylonian captivity. They have been there now for over fifty years. There is hardly a survivor left who can remember what being close to God was like. There is hardly one still living who can remember vividly what it was like being in Jerusalem or near the Holy City. They had forgotten what it was like to be near God at Mount Moriah. They had been fifty years without any effective prayer life and communication with God, to the extent that they were not quite sure what it would be like — and not sure whether that was what they wanted. Now the prophet was saying to them, "Hey, the Persian king has now conquered Babylon. We prayed that God would answer our prayer and set us free that we might turn back to God, back to the Promised Land, and Cyrus is the answer to prayer. Now you have an opportunity to go back to a nearness with God. You can turn back to a relationship with him, back to Jerusalem, back to the Promised Land." But do not forget that they had been gone for fifty years. That was home . . . they were natives. That made them original "old family." They had been living that lifestyle for fifty years and had been getting along pretty well without God. So, some of them wondered, "Well, why should I go out there in this strange wilderness trying this new kind of relationship with God when I am not even sure it is there? I have never been there. How do we know it will work and we can live there and once again be close to God in that Holy Place?

They had a lot of questions about it. But the prophet says, a new relationship is possible. This is how ne explains you can have that new relationship. Isaiah 55:10-13 cannot be studied or understood unless we also include verses six to nine in the reading. To those who are not quite sure it is what they want, to those who are not quite sure how you get it, to those who have perhaps never had it, he explains when you should pray.

I. When

Isaiah writes: "Seek the Lord while he is near. Call upon Him while he may be found," now what he is saying is that silence is the answer to prayer. We have prayer at our disposal, there is no use remaining in the same kind of condition in our life and family any longer. The time to start praying is right now! "Seek him while he is near." Do not say, "Tomorrow I am going to start trying to pray." *Start right now!* Do not say, "Tomorrow I am going to set out on a new journey to the Promised Land, back to a close relationship with God." No, you start it now! "Seek the Lord while he is near. Call upon him while he may be found."

"Found" and "near" imply that you can discover him. You are not going to discover him tomorrow but now. He is a *living,* a *now* God. You are not going to find him in the past. You are going to find him now, *right now.* He is saying that you need to draw apart from the world. Those are the graphic symbols of "found" and "near". You must respond now if you are to get out of the kind of lifestyles in which you are trapped.

Jesus says, "When you pray, get into your closet." Do you know what a closet is? We used to call bathrooms or outhouses closets when I was a boy, but that is not what Isaiah has in mind. A closet in the Bible was a dressing room off from the temple where priests changed their clothes. They disrobed to dress in order to enter the temple. They had to put on certain attire. It was the place where you stripped naked. You take off your $200 suit. You take off your $100 dress. You take off all your superficialities, all your pretense, all your masks, all your aggressiveness, all your success. You take it off and get down just like you were when you came in this world. You disrobe. You go in your closet where there is no pretension and you find him and he finds you.

We approach everything else the same way we do prayer. You have had an aggressive day at the office and you tell your wife you will meet her at the box office to attend a concert; but, if you go to that concert with the same kind of attitude and the same kind of technique with which you have approached the whole day, you are going to be miserable. If you go in there aggressively, you are not going to get anything out of it. You have to change your techniques. You have to go in there in a receptive mood, do you not? You have to go while allowing something to be done to you and for you through the music. You have to leave the world in which you are trying to do *for* the world and *to* the world, and allow the music to do something *to you*.

That is what prayer is! You go in that robing room and you disrobe and you take off that old, selfish kind of "pushy", aggressive, "go-getter" attitude. Most of us pray that way. We "go after it." We are aggressive people. "Lord, help me; do this for me." And we approach God totally that way. We live by the philosophy that the squeaking wheel gets the grease. So we assume that if we squeak enough and loud enough, the Lord is going to hear. We try to manipulate him.

Our church services in Greenville. North Carolina were broadcast on the radio. The angriest reply I ever got from that large radio audience was a letter from an unemployed clergyman who was home in bed. He wrote an extremely aggressive letter, responding to my sermon, one in which I mentioned something about the effectiveness of prayer. He said, "I tried it. I prayed, and God did not do all I wanted him to do and what I asked him to do." You could feel the hostility in that letter. But Jesus prayed, "Not my will but thy will be done," which is an entirely different technique.

I do not have a lot of regular time for prayer, but one such time I have is in the morning after I run six miles. There is one particular chair in which my wife will allow me to sit when I am still perspiring with a sweatsuit on. I sit there and read and pray. I am physically exhausted. That is the best time. As Paul says in 2 Corinthians, "As the physical becomes weaker and weaker, the inner man becomes stronger and stronger." What he means is that all this aggressiveness, this outward exterior, is weakened at that moment; the spiritual man has a stronger opportunity to take over. The barriers that you set up, the things with which you shield your soul, all the material aggressiveness of the world — when all of it is down, then you can spiritually relate. This is the whole purpose of the Indian religion's philosophy of yoga and the other physical disciplines that go along with prayer: Yu are subdued; the body, the physical, the material are set aside, that your spiritual and inner self might take over.

II. How Do You Pray

The prophet says, "Let the wicked forsake his ways and the unrighteous man his thoughts. Let him return to the Lord, that He may have mercy upon him; and to God, for he will abundantly pardon; for my thoughts are not your thoughts, neither are my ways your ways. As the Heavens are higher than the earth, so are my thoughts higher than your thoughts and my ways than your ways, saith the Lord."

Forsake your unrighteous thoughts. "Let him forsake his own way and his own will." That is the only way prayer takes place — when you surrender your will to God's will. This is the process of praying. Most of us, when we pray, have already decided what our problem is. Maybe it is one of your children. Maybe it is your job. Maybe it is your marriage. You decide what you think the answer is and you get down on your knees and pray, "God, grant this. Do it!" What you are really saying is, "Now, Lord, you do not know too much about your business, but I know best. Just do what I want." We ask him for the answer rather than give him the problem, because we think our answer to the problem is better than his answer to the problem. "Let the wicked man forsake his thoughts and his own way and will, saith the Lord".

Sometimes I talk so much that the Lord just does not have a chance to say anything. Do you ever do that? And he is trying to say something but he cannot get a word in edgewise. My wife bought me a hat to match a topcoat once, and I lost the hat in the airport in Chicago. I got home and it was still snowing and I needed a hat. I went to the haberdashers mith whom I normally traded. They were Jewish men and close personal friends of mine. I had bought all my clothing from them for years, but they did not have a hat like I was looking for. So, I went to a different store, belonging to another Jewish gentleman. He had the exact hat for which I was looking. But, I had never traded with him and was a little skeptical about him. I always liked to bargain with people so I said, "How much will you take for it?" He said, "Try it on." I said, "How much will you take for it? What wears good with me is how much it costs." He said, "Do you like it?" I said, "How much is it?" "Put it on," he said, "Do you like it. Reverend?" I thought to myself, "I am going to get taken," but I put it on and I liked it. It was a perfect fit. I said, "How much?" He said. "It's yours. I want to give it to you." Boy, did I ever feel small! I almost disappeared.

That is the way I have been reacting to God, always worrying about what kind of deal I am going to make when he is trying to do something for me and I will not let him. That is the way most of us react. And then, too, when he says, "Let the wicked forsake his ways and the unrighteous man his thoughts," it is not so obvious that we are always selfish. Some of our prayers are not obviously selfish. For example, we might pray for protection and security, which may mean for you freedom from worry about the future and your professional survival, when God might have a different idea about what *He* means by security. Or, you might pray for your children's success in school, when God's idea of what success for your children might be would be entirely different from what your idea might be. Or you might pray, "Lord, I'm lonely and abandoned," and you forget that Jesus was abandoned and lonely. Let the wicked forsake his way and the unrighteous man his thoughts. But, here is the key: Isaiah 55:10-11.

III. Why

Why will prayer always work 100 percent of the time? Prayer that works emphasizes not your words but God's, emphasizing not your words to him (that is of no consequence), but *his words to you*. Let me share this verse from Isaiah with you. I think it is poetic.

For as the rain and the snow come down from Heaven and return not thither but water the earth making it bring forth and sprout, making seed to the soil and bread to the eater, so shall my word be that goes forth from my mouth. It shall not ever return to me empty, never. It shall always accomplish that which I purpose and in all things it shall prosper for what I sent it.

You and I put too much emphasis on the power of our words and too little on God's Word. God's Word will never return empty — never. Not my will but Thine be done. This is how you can have the assurance that prayer will always work — when you put your emphasis on God's Word. His Word always accomplishes that which he purposes. It never returns empty. Often when I pray, my words just come back empty. But, God's word never does. It accomplishes that which he intends. That is why the Lord's prayer ends with: "For Thine is the kingdom and the power." *Thine:* that is the whole answer to prayer. When the disciples said. "Lord, teach us how to pray," Jesus taught them the Lord's Prayer and ended, "For Thine is the kingdom and the power." That is where the success is: Thine. the submission and surrender to let him reign and his word succeed in our lives.

I went into our chapel a few weeks ago and there was a college girl, sitting by herself in prayer. I walked up to her and asked, "May I help you?" She raised up from her knees with a glow in her face and said, "Thank you, but I am being helped."

My word shall not ever return unto me empty. Whatever I prosper it to be, it shall be. Whatever I intended to accomplish, it shall accomplish. It shall never return unto me empty."

Exodus 34:29-35   Transfiguration (Common, Lutheran)

How to Get a Glow on Your Face

Last week I read a book on tne religious life of William James, the author of *The Varieties of Religious Experience.* James was greatly influenced by his scholarly father, Henry, and agreed with him on everything except "that empirical truth is the only truth there is." William James contended that "experience" was the supreme knowledge and also the only unrefutable fact. We live in a world that has been profoundly influenced by James, making us aware of the endless possibilities of new knowledge by experience.

You can "prove" Christianity or the existence of God empirically. It can be done, no question about it. That's what we call "head faith." But your faith never really comes alive until you have *experienced* him, whose existence you have proven. Nothing takes the place of experience.

Every week, I have people come to me in the office and say, "If I could only have an experience like some of the people with whom I have talked. If I could only have a first-hand encounter with the ever-living Christ, then I could embrace him intellectually. It would change my life." Every week, I meet people who have believed in the Bible as infallible proof of God's Word and who recently have had an experience with Christ and suddenly now they are "turned on." They still believe the same things, but now it is real to them.

Until I studied this passage from Exodus, I believed that some people just "have an experience" with God and some people don't. I concluded the reason was that some people just have a different psychological makeup; they are just more inclined to an unexperiential kind of faith. That perhaps they are a little more emotional, or personal, or whatever. However, that's not what the Bible says. Paul wrote, "If you have not had an experience with Jesus Christ, it means you are among those perishing." Paul goes on to say, "the evil force of this world veils your eyes" like sunglasses, so that you do not see God face to face and, therefore you reason that kind of experience doesn't really exist. Paul says that the "god of this world" has blinded the minds of those who haven't had the experience, to keep them from seeing the light of the gospel of the glory of Christ, which is in the likeness of God.

The Gospel of Matthew records that Jesus on the Mount of Transfiguration had the same kind of experiences as did Moses on Sinai. It says, "Jesus taking James, John, and Peter went up on Mount. Hermon and there was transfigured." Once they had this experience with God, Jesus looked different. It was as if his clothes were of "shining raiment." Matthew explains why it is that some people have an experience and some don't. Notice, Jesus had twelve or more disciples, but only three of them, Peter, James and John, had the experience of seeing God transfigured in Jesus. The reason was that there were only three who had the veil of the eyes taken away, so that they could see. Note also that they became the main leaders of Christianity after the resurrection and the creating of the Church.

You can read about thousands of experiences. You can read all of them that William James records in *The Varieties of Religious Experience.* In every case, we identify them as illumination, meaning that it was a light that came. Paul described his as a light from heaven. Every religious experience is always defined as illumination. No two would be alike. Yours should not be like mine or Paul's, but James says that everyone will experience God face to face, whose eyes are not veiled by the veils of this world. If you haven't experienced, it isn't because you are not inclined that way, it is because your eyes have been veiled and you have not seen him face to face.

The light of the Shekinah was God's glory being communicated to Moses. This account is the antetype of the account of the Transfiguration of Jesus as recorded in the gospels. Moses' religious experience was obvious to Aaron and the people as valid and holy, because of the presence of light shining in his face. Priests in that period of Bible history always wore a veil over their face before going before God or being in his presence. It is noteworthy here that Moses was the first man recorded in the Bible to take off his veil in the presence of God. The verb translated "shone" occurs only twice in Hebrew literature, here and in Psalm 69:31. In the latter account, the verb is used as a bullock displaying horns. The word is derived from the noun "horn." The vulgate translates it "horned;" hence the representation of the old painters and Michelangelo of Moses with horns. In Job 3:4, "horns" denotes rays of light or lightening flashes. This explains the "light" or "shining faces" used throughout history to explain a person's real conversion or spiritual experience or encounter with the everliving God. Moses' mountaintop illumination affirms the two fundamentals of all religious experience:

I. Light and Illumination is Basic in all Religious Experience

Many of you have read Raymond Moody's best seller, *Life After Life*. Some claim that it will sell more than any other book printed in the twentieth century. He wrote most of it while he was teaching Sunday church school in the congregation I served for the past ten years. It was a collection of medical records from, and interviews with scientists and physicians around the world, clinically recorded, of people who died, were pronounced clinically dead, and who then came back to life. Moody has been on the "Today" show, and several other network shows and lectured on university campuses across our land. In this book he records the religious experiences of hundreds. A large portion of the people interviewed were previously non-believers.

All of them experienced a bright light. That was the most significant thing — a bright light. All of these persons said they went through a dark tunnel where they could see a dim light at the end and, the closer they got to it, the brighter it became. They all described it as a light beyond comprehension, brighter than any light they had ever before seen, and yet it didn't hurt their eyes. It was wonderful, and it was comforting. They all said it was not exactly a definite beam, but it was a definite personality, like the glory of someone's countenance. They all said that the presence of that person's thoughts were transferred to their mind automatically, as if they knew what he knew and he knew what they knew, and nothing was hidden anymore. It was total illumination.

Now I hope you don't make the mistake of thinking that, because there is darkness in the world, that is reason to be depressed or pessimistic. When the Bible describes how the world is filled with darkness, that is the basis for hope. The light is not light if there is no darkness. Light cannot even be distinguishable if there is no darkness. The worshiping of the Golden Calf demonstrates the darkness in which the children of Israel walked — hence the need for the light. Life after death would mean nothing if there was no death. Light wouldn't mean anything unless there was darkness. And that is our hope.

In 1910 the ship *Republic* was in the process of sinking. Another ship, the *Baltic,* was dispatched to try and rescue the people from the *Republic.* All day long the *Baltic* circled the *Republic* but could not see it. In the fog, they could not see the ship. But as the sun set, the people on the wounded *Republic* knew that their chances of survival were now gone, and they could never be saved because darkness had come. But, in the darkness the *Baltic* was able to see the lights of the sinking ship and to rescue all the passengers. It could not be seen in the daytime, but the light was visible only at night. This is hope. In spite of the fact that the world is filled with millions of miles of darkness into outer space, even that cannot snuff out the light that comes in the transfigured face of Jesus.

II. Light Transfiguration

Light always transfigures. That is why we call the experience of seeing God face to face on Mount Hermon "the Transfiguration." Matthew says that Jesus' whole countenance was altered, his raiment was "dazzling white". I looked up the word "transfigure" and Webster says it means "to recognize in an object or a person or an event a reality of another order, of a different kind. The familiar is changed. The appearance of the familiar is changed so the reality and meaning heretofore unsuspected is revealed." That which you have seen, the common, suddenly takes on a new meaning.

Moses explains transfiguration as the light shining to reveal the glory of God. Moses was still the same Moses who had walked among them, but now he was transfigured. They saw the glory of God in him.

When I was a boy, I remember some of the country people talking about their religious experiences. They would say, "I've got glory, glory" meaning they had seen him, who, before in their experience had been the historical Jesus, but who now became God, omnipotent. The change takes place. It is not mere illumination as you and

I mean illumination. By illumination you and I mean "shining a spotlight on something so that it better reveals it," like a spotlight shining on your desk. No, the Bible talks about the kind of illumination that comes from within, not outside. The inner skin of Moses shone. The light is that which comes from within to the outside. You can see it. It is not that which is from outside.

The movie "E.T." is the story of a friendship between E.T., who is a ten-million-year-old extra-terrestrial creature and a ten-year-old boy named Elliot. E.T. is hardly a candidate for a hero in most movies. In our world we put so much importance on appearance, on people looking like us and being glamorous. E.T.'s appearance is a cross between a wrinkled bullfrog and a mushroom. He decides to inhabit a house which is certainly not a model Christian home. The mother has just been separated from the father, the children stay up as late as they want to and talk about whatever they want to and swear and curse. It seems to be nothing but confusion in this house, yet E.T., the creature from outer space, comes in and touches something very basic in the human spirit. Suddenly, that which before had been ordinary becomes illuminated. In an age of violence, gratuitous sex and confusion, E.T. brings a message of love, risky caring and communication. When E.T. falls ill and the American government decides they have to do away with this creature, nobody could see him as Elliot could. E.T. was dying. What was it that brought him back to life again? It was that unconditional love that the children felt for this strange, weird-looking creature. And suddenly that love, like a light inside of him, began to glow. A healing power flowed through his whole body and he was healed by this glow.

So it was in Jesus' day. The government of his day never saw Jesus as he really was. They saw him as one who was "different" and, because he was different, they had to put him to death. But others who had the vision who had had the experience, the transfiguration, now saw him entirely differently. They saw him as the Savior, as the Messiah.

Yes, light transfigures. God's glow and light transfigured Moses and it can put the same glow on your face.